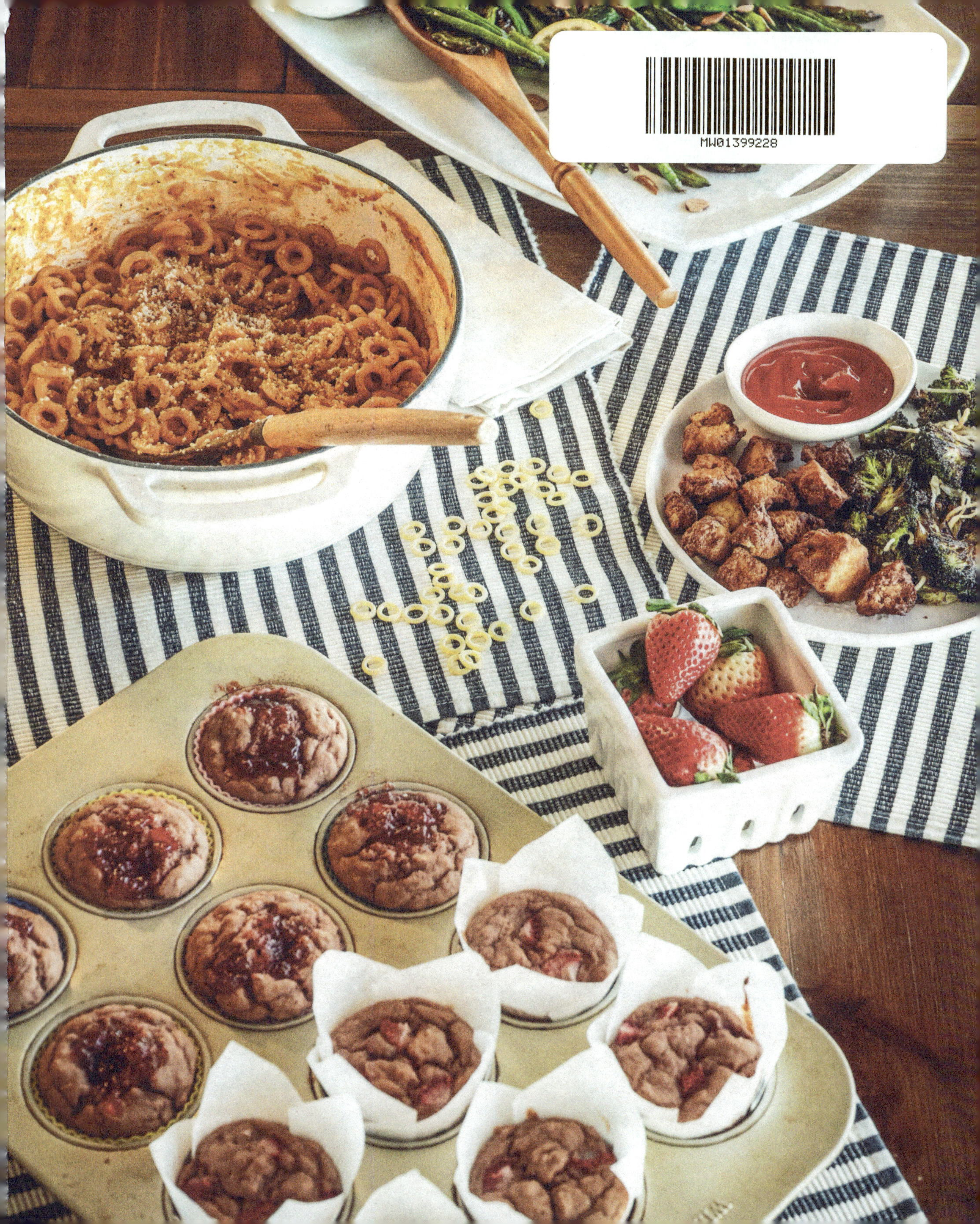

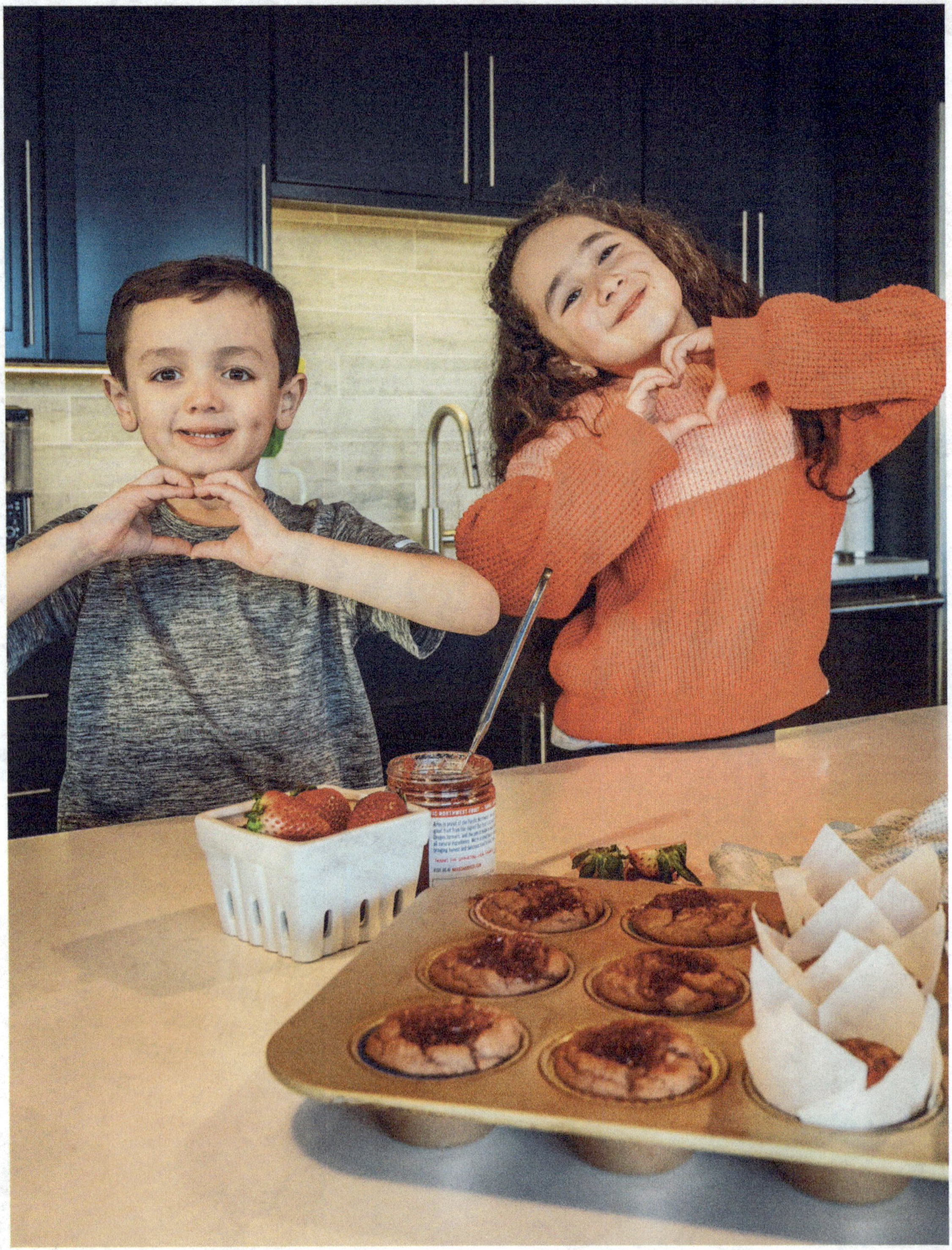

Cooking Healthy
For the Family

Over 75 **Plant-Focused** Recipes
Everyone In The Family Will Enjoy

Elaina Moon, BS, Certified Health Coach

Copyright © 2023 Elaina Moon
All rights reserved.

Dedication

To the One that makes this all possible. This book is a celebration of the love of family, the love of cooking, and the love flowing through generations. May this book be a blessing to you and yours.

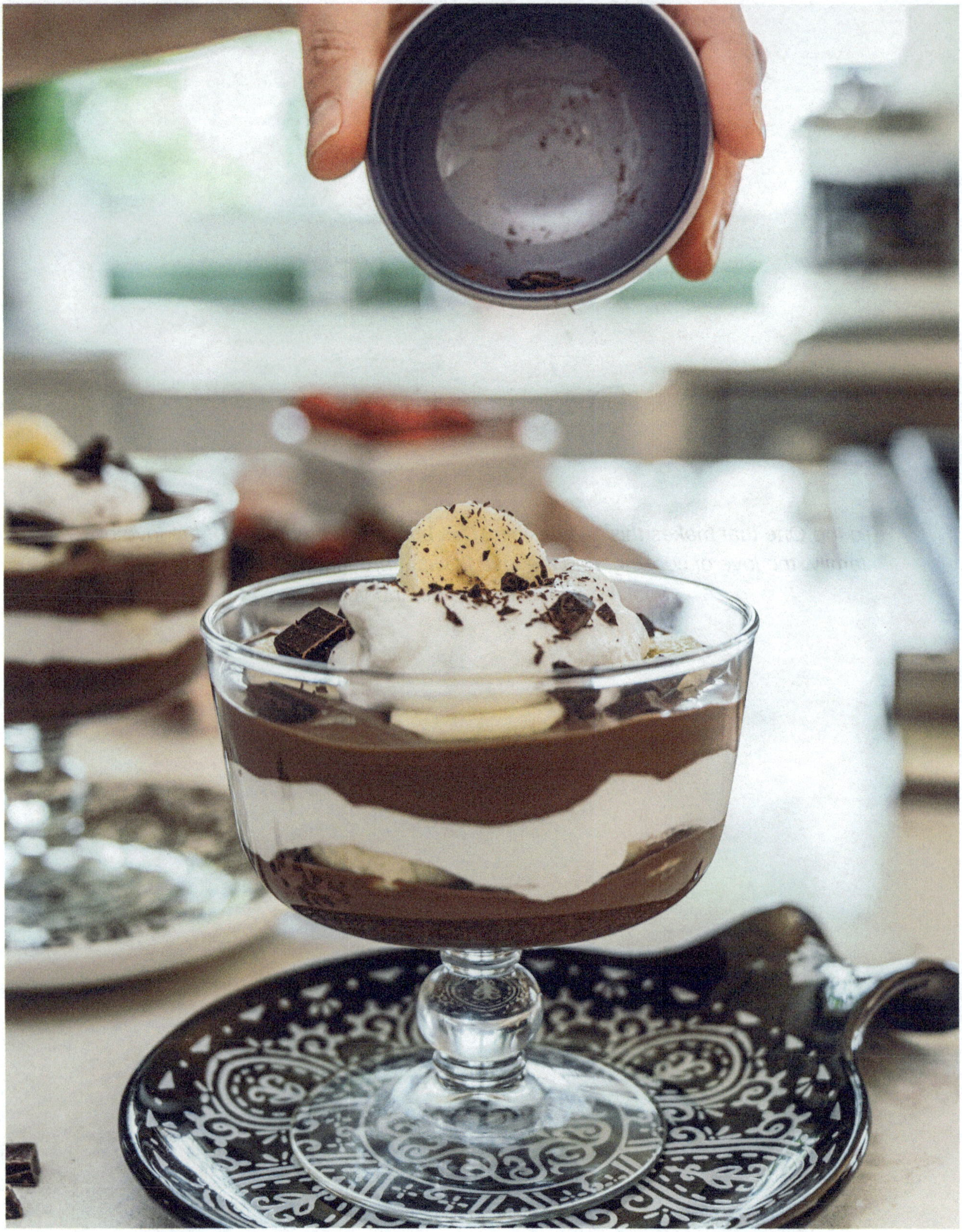

Contents

Foreword 8

Cooking Healthy For The Family 10

10 Tips For Feeding Your Family 12

10 Tips For Navigating Recipes With Ease 14

CH 1 Bright Mornings 17

CH 2 Snack Attack 43

CH 3 Veggie Loaded 65

CH 4 Adventurous Eaters 87

CH 5 Warm Soups 105

CH 6 Entrée Pastas 119

CH 7 Beans and Lentils 135

CH 8 Sweet Treats 153

Acknowledgments 170

About the Author 173

Foreword

I recently heard a podcast discussing the key to lifelong happiness. The podcast was only eight minutes long; you'd think with this topic, it would be a much longer discussion. But the truth is, when we think about what makes us truly, genuinely happy, the list is short. The podcast shared that the key to happiness is being fully present and surrounded by the people we love, and I agree.

When Elaina discussed with me the premise of this book, I loved the idea immediately. A cookbook full of recipes that encourages families to join around the kitchen island; chopping, stirring, laughing, making genuine memories and colorful delicious plates? Yes please. It's wonderful that this cookbook stirs in us a desire for a simple, yet fulfilling time. Time not wasted.

Elaina, along with being a teacher, chef, and health coach, is also a mom. At certain points, we parents realize how quickly our children are growing. Though right in front of our eyes, we don't see it happening until we look back at pictures or notice their toppling heights. It's in these moments when we think, "Where did the time go?"

In a world where busyness and a checked-off to-do list are considered markers of success, I love the idea of tossing aside the to-do list, putting on an apron with our kids, and creating a messy kitchen. Years from now, we won't look back and think about how messy our kitchens did, in fact, get. We'll be grateful for those endearing moments that brought us closer as a family, with no agenda; just good food, laughter, and joy. And those will be some of our kids' favorite memories too, and that's priceless.

Carol Taylor, MPH, RD, Certified Diabetes Care and Education Specialist, Health Coach, friend, and mom of three littles

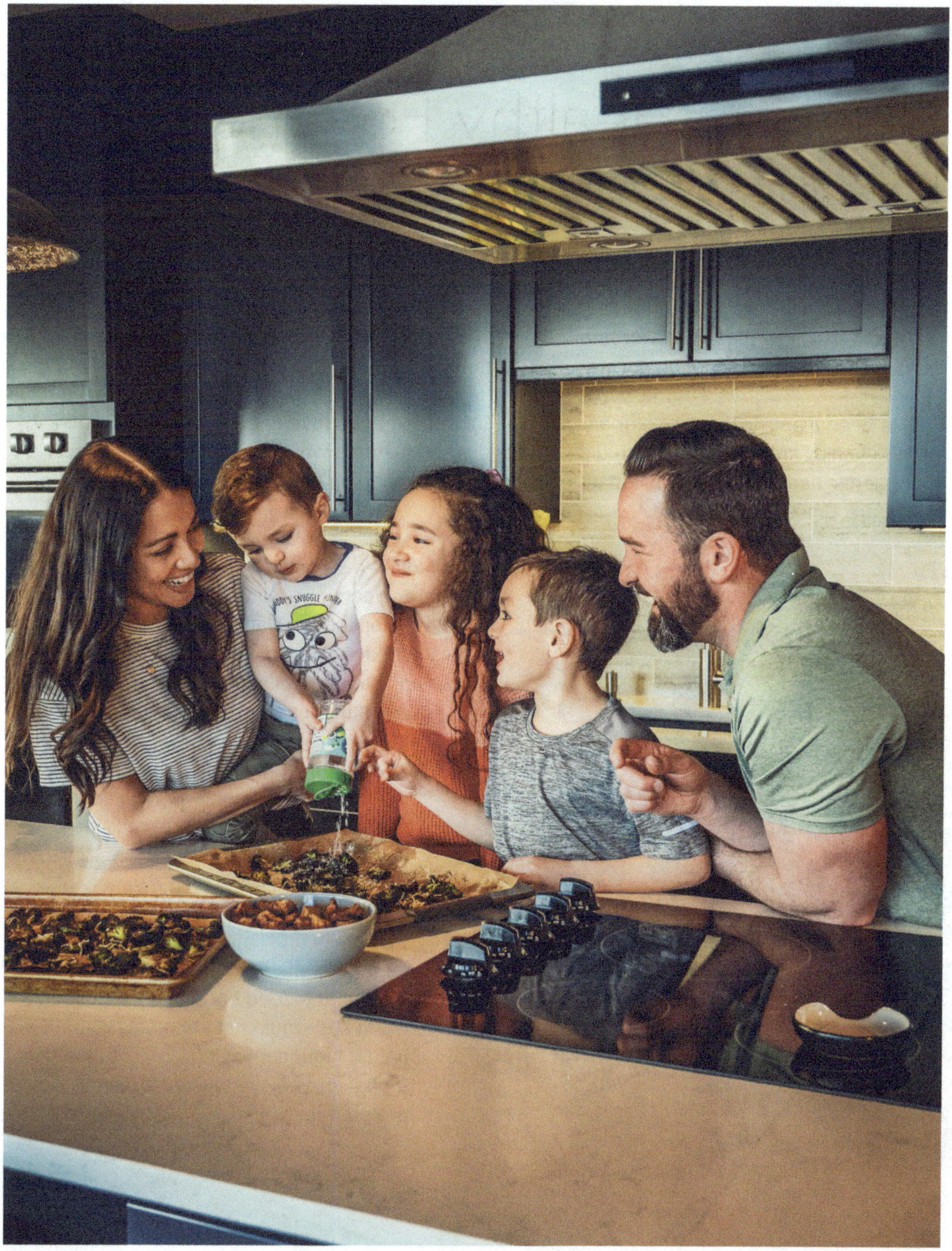

Cooking Healthy For The Family
How I learned to feed my family

Preparing a meal for a family is a wonderful and fulfilling act of love. While I enjoy watching my family devour a meal, feeding them comes with challenges. While we have the best intentions of offering our family healthy meals, life, lack of time, pickiness, and food preferences sometimes get in the way. We get excited for another opportunity to feed them something good, only to get frustrated when it does not go our way. I have been there. Trust me, you are not alone.

I have been a passionate cook for as long as I can remember. I love to cook and enjoy teaching others. I enjoy creating meals with different flavors and textures while experimenting with new ingredients. I enjoy the satisfaction of feeding others and seeing their reactions to what I make, which are almost always good.

However, my kitchen creativity came to a screeching halt almost three years ago with a new addition to our family. Adopting our daughter changed our world for the better. But every new change requires an adjustment. Let's just say I didn't take this adjustment to my cooking very well.

This change came as a whirlwind during the first COVID year, and while we were overjoyed, we did not quite anticipate all the challenges that would arise. While my husband and I like eating a variety of foods, our new daughter did not. She was very picky and limited on foods she would put on her plate. I found myself struggling with what to feed her and disappointed when she would not eat meals without a battle. I found myself giving in to the "kid foods" she enjoyed just to appease her preferences.

While that challenge was difficult, it brought my cooking creativity to a beautiful new place. One without the expectation of perfection. A place of understanding how to modify and incorporate foods that she accepted. We are now in a new place, where she is comfortable trying things, exploring more foods, and even enjoying them!

This book is my journey to a new way to feed my family. My desire is that it inspires you to get out of your routine and try something new. I hope it gives you the encouragement you need to keep trying. I hope you know that you are not alone. Whether you have young kids or teens, are an empty nester, or are enjoying the golden years, rest assured there is something here for you. Included in this cookbook are simple, delicious, and satisfying recipes you will keep in your back pocket and refer to over and over again.

Most of all, I pray you feel the love that went into this book — the love shared by family.

Happy Cooking & God Bless,

Elaina Moon, Certified Health Coach and Cooking Class Instructor
Wife, mom, business owner, and foodie

10 Tips For Feeding Your Family

1 — Allow your family to make choices.

There are many ways to involve the whole family in making a meal, from planning to cooking. Any opportunity to get them involved will deepen their connection to what is nourishing their bodies. Growing a garden or just herbs inside, looking through cookbooks together, and letting them choose the vegetables for the week are just a few ways to create connection.

2 — Exposure is an important first step.

Exposing kids to healthy foods is a great first step. Watching you enjoy healthy foods will help increase their curiosity and hopefully they will decide to try the foods for themselves. You are their role model for healthy eating. What you do and say about food will impact their perception the most!

3 — Introduce new flavors to foods they already enjoy.

I love cooking with spices and herbs. Instead of adding them to new foods, start by using them with something they already love, like potatoes or rice. Let them smell and taste the herb or spice on its own first to help them accept the new ingredient.

4 — Lower your expectations.

In a perfect world, our families will eat what is in front of them all the time and not complain. I don't live in that world, and I assume you don't either. Developing a good relationship with food is more important than forcing bites. This takes time, even into adulthood. Be patient and don't expect that they will be amazing eaters right now. They will get there with support.

5 — Serve foods you know they like.

Instead of cooking a separate meal, offer one or two items at each meal you know they will like. For everything else, ask for a polite bite and allow them to make the choice to have more.

6 — Put those leftovers to good use.

We have a leftover night in our house where it all comes out and my family gets to choose what they are putting on their plates. It doesn't have to go together, be the same cuisine, or even have to include every food group in order to be a meal. Those are the best times for you to encourage individual autonomy.

7 — Keep healthy ready-to-eat foods on hand.

While I enjoy a freshly cooked meal most nights, it's not realistic with a busy schedule. Keep ready-to-eat foods on hand to round out a meal. Some examples include: frozen cooked grains, canned beans, fresh washed fruit, raw cut-up veggies, healthy sauces, dips, and pre-cooked proteins.

8 — Boost nutrition with small changes.

Try adding small pieces of new foods to already loved dishes. Minced cooked carrots can be added to rice, or like-colored vegetables can be blended into broths or sauces. I love adding beans to ground proteins, such as lentils mixed in with taco filling. They are a hearty addition and eaters already enjoy taco flavors. Check out the loaded veggie section for more ideas!

9 — Camouflage what you can.

I love adding veggies to sauces and liquids. This can be done by grinding them up in a food processor or blending them into a liquid or sauce. When the timing is right, tell your family what is in the meal. Understanding what they are eating will help improve their relationship with food. Play a guessing game of what is in the meal and see who can get the most right!

10 — Add variety without the effort.

I enjoy serving simple things that I know my daughter will eat and that do not involve much prep or cooking. Some ideas are whole or cut-up fruits, raw veggies, roasted veggies, nuts, or healthy crackers or chips. Don't exclude foods if they don't "go with" the meal served. Serving options they like will help your family feel more comfortable about any new foods that are in front of them.

10 Tips For Navigating Recipes With Ease

Measurements

tsp = teaspoon
tbsp = tablespoon
dry ingredients = dry measuring cups and spoons
wet ingredients = liquid measuring cup

1 — Substitutions

Most recipes in this book can be modified for gluten-free, dairy-free, egg-free, and other replacements. Alternative options for recipes are specified in the recipe's tip section. Some recipes cannot be made egg-free because the alternatives available will not yield a good final product.

2 — Cooking, Product, and Modification Tips

Recipes have tips below the nutrition facts to help you cook through the recipe and answer common questions. Recipes can be adjusted to fit your family's tastes and preferences. Be sure to read the tips before starting the recipe.

3 — Invest in a Good Blender and Food Processor

I use these two appliances many times a week and they are often used in these recipes to speed up the prep work. They are essential for blending vegetables into sauces, soups, and other veggie-loaded dishes. I love my Vitamix blender and Hamilton Beach food processor. You can find many inexpensive options as well.

4 — Pre-Minced vs. Fresh Garlic

Some of the recipes will indicate which one to use. If you are making a recipe where the garlic will not be cooked, I prefer pre-minced for a milder taste. If the garlic will be cooked, either one is an option, but the fresh will give you a better garlic flavor in the end.

5 — Read the Recipe Before Getting Started

Getting acquainted with the recipe is important for understanding the steps involved before any cooking happens. This will help with time management as well. Read the recipe, then start gathering ingredients and equipment.

6 — Mise En Place

Mise en place is a French culinary term meaning "everything in its place". In my kitchen, this is essential for a tidy and organized workspace. Students in my classroom are instructed to not turn on any heat until all the ingredients, equipment, and prep work has been done. The ingredient list will have prepping instructions for each listed ingredient. Being organized will not only save you time but keep the cooking experience more enjoyable for everyone. Prepping the ingredients for a meal is a great way to get the kids in the kitchen!

7 — Garnish and Toppings

Some recipes in this book have garnish and topping suggestions. These are optional. For adults and kids with a wider range of tastes, using a garnish or topping is one way to boost flavor and interest. However, picky kids might prefer these to be on the side or left out completely.

8 — Spices and Herbs

Fresh herbs aren't as strong in flavor as dried, so you will want to use more if substituting. Dried herbs and spices shouldn't be kept for longer than a year, as they will lose their flavor over time. Dried herbs can be rubbed between your fingers to release the oil and bring out more flavor.

9 — Types of Oils

There are different kinds of oils used for cooking. Neutral oils are those without flavor and can be heated to a higher temperature without burning. Healthier forms of those oils include avocado, grapeseed, light olive, safflower, and organic vegetable or canola. Other oils add flavor or dilute dressings, such as sesame and extra virgin olive oils.

10 — Added Sugars

Most of the recipes in this book have healthier alternative sugars like coconut sugar, maple syrup, agave, honey, and molasses. In most cases, you can substitute coconut sugar for white or brown sugar. Maple syrup, agave, and honey are interchangeable. Some recipes identify a specific liquid sweetener because of the flavor it imparts to the dish. Remember that some recipes, like my French Apple Cake, need white sugar for texture and color. Therefore, other sugars cannot be substituted. Be sure to check out the tips for each recipe before making substitutions.

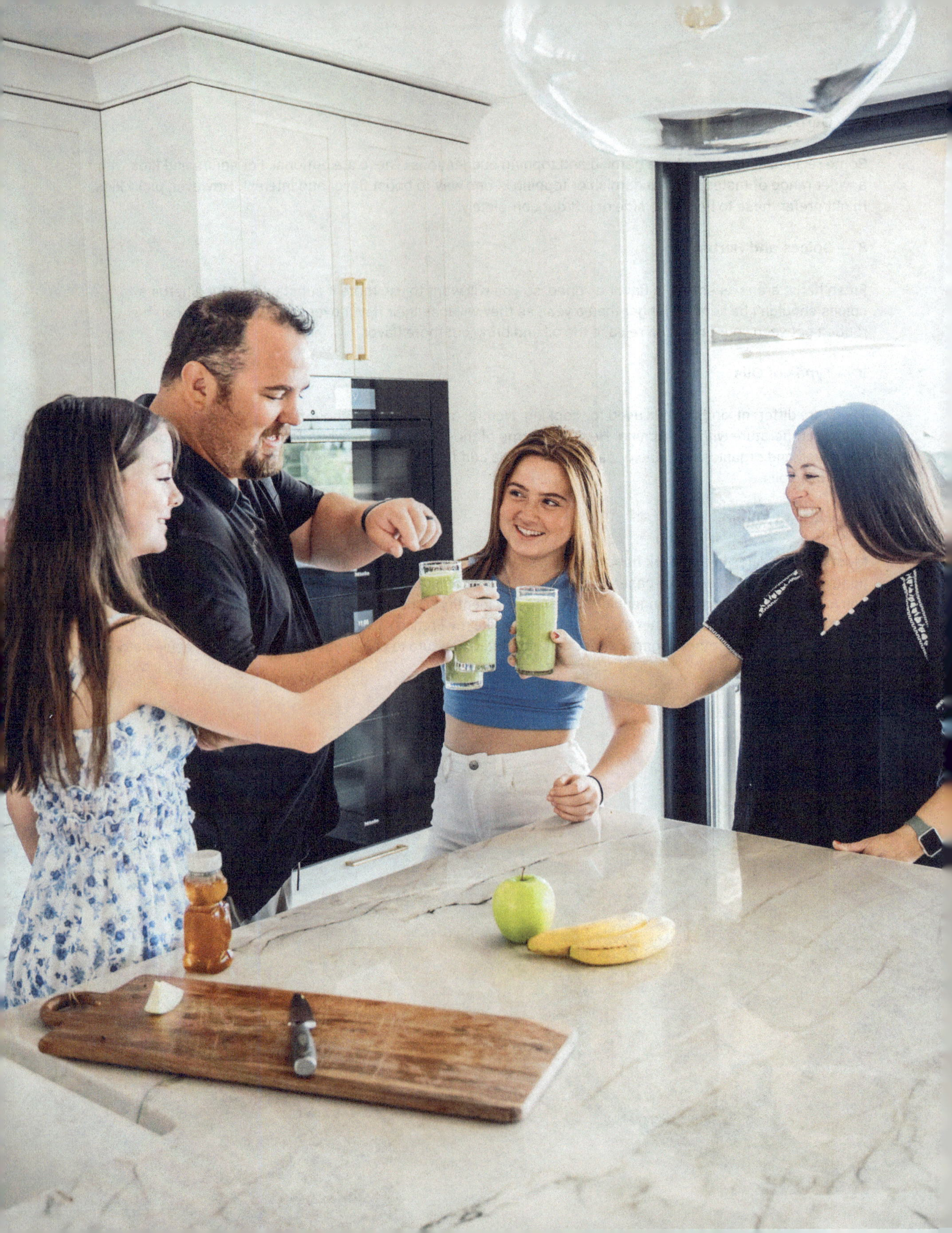

Bright Mornings

Apple Pie Baked Oatmeal	**19**
Chocolate Chia Pudding	**20**
Orange Cranberry Baked Apples	**22**
Hash Brown Waffles	**23**
Creamy Style Potato Pancakes	**25**
Sisters Apple Sauce	**27**
Strawberry Smoothie Muffins	**28**
Pumpkin Chocolate Oat Muffins	**31**
Double Chocolate Zucchini Muffins	**33**
Green Protein Smoothie	**34**
Green Veggie Pancakes	**37**
Chunky Monkey Granola	**39**
Eggy Veggie Muffins	**40**

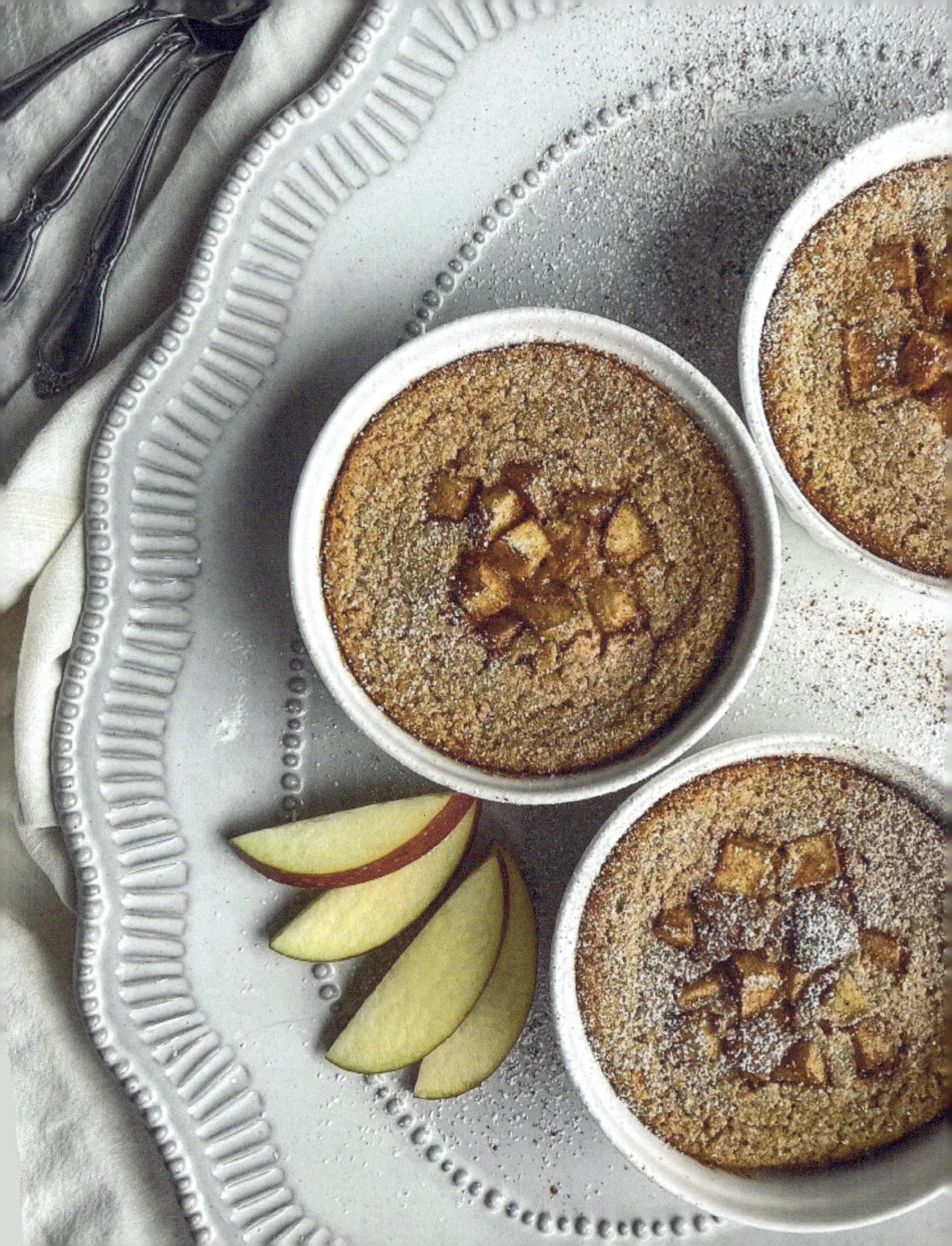

Apple Pie Baked Oatmeal

For cozy fall or winter mornings, this recipe is perfect. But don't stop there! It comes together so quickly, you can make it for a quick weekday breakfast, a hearty snack for older kids and teens, or even lunch to take to work. Get the kids in the kitchen with you on this one and practice measuring skills!

SERVES 4, 1/4 of recipe per serving

Cooking spray

1 cup old-fashioned oats

1/4 cup unsweetened applesauce

2 tbsp melted butter of choice

1 tsp baking powder

1/4 cup maple syrup

1 cup unsweetened dairy-free or regular milk

1 tbsp pure vanilla extract

1 egg or flax egg (1 tbsp ground flaxseed mixed with 2 1/2 tbsp water)

1/2 tsp pumpkin pie spice

1/2 tsp ground cinnamon

1/8 tsp ground cloves

1/8 tsp ground nutmeg

Pinch of salt

Toppings

1/2 cup small diced red or green baking apple

1/4 tsp ground cinnamon

1 tsp lemon juice

1 tsp brown sugar or coconut sugar
milk of choice, optional for serving

Preheat the oven to 400 degrees and spray four, 4-inch ramekins with cooking spray.

Add all the oatmeal ingredients to a blender and blend until it's well combined with only small pieces; think chunky baby food consistency.

Add all the topping ingredients to a small bowl and mix together.

Pour the batter evenly between the four ramekins and top with apple mixture. Place all four ramekins on a baking sheet.

Bake for 18–20 minutes or until the top feels set. Serve hot with warm milk of choice, optional.

🛒 PRODUCT TIP

A few common baking apples include: Granny Smith, Honeycrisp, Fuji, Gala, Honey Gold, and a new favorite of mine, Cosmic Crisp.

🍲 COOKING TIP

Using the baking sheet under the ramekins makes for easy handling in and out of the oven. For serving to kids, make sure to cool the ramekins or you can transfer the oatmeal to a bowl.

Calories 241 | Carbs 37g | Fat 9g | Protein 5g | Fiber 4g | Sodium 66mg

Chocolate Chia Pudding

A simple make-ahead breakfast or snack, this can be used for a sweet treat too! Top with fresh berries, mini chocolate chips, or even whipped cream for a healthy decadence!

SERVES 4, 1/3 cup per serving

15 oz canned light coconut milk, shaken

3 tbsp pure maple syrup

½ tbsp pure vanilla extract

1 - 2 tbsp unsweetened cocoa powder

3 tbsp hazelnut or white chocolate creamer of choice

⅓ cup chia seeds

Topping Options
Shredded coconut, sliced strawberries or bananas, mini chocolate chips, chocolate syrup, whipped cream

In a bowl, add all the ingredients, except the toppings, and whisk well. Let sit for 5 minutes, then whisk again to break up any clumps.

Store in the bowl or transfer to a mason jar and refrigerate overnight or for at least 8 hours to thicken. Divide into four bowls and garnish with toppings of choice.

COOKING TIPS

Start with 1 tablespoon of cocoa powder, then taste to see if the extra tablespoon is needed.

The creamer helps the pudding keep a delicious creaminess. Use whatever brand and flavor you like that will complement the chocolate.

MODIFICATION TIP

Don't have canned coconut milk? You can substitute 1 ½ cups of any milk.

Without toppings
Calories 197 | Carbs 19g | Fat 11g | Protein 4g | Fiber 7g | Sodium 10mg

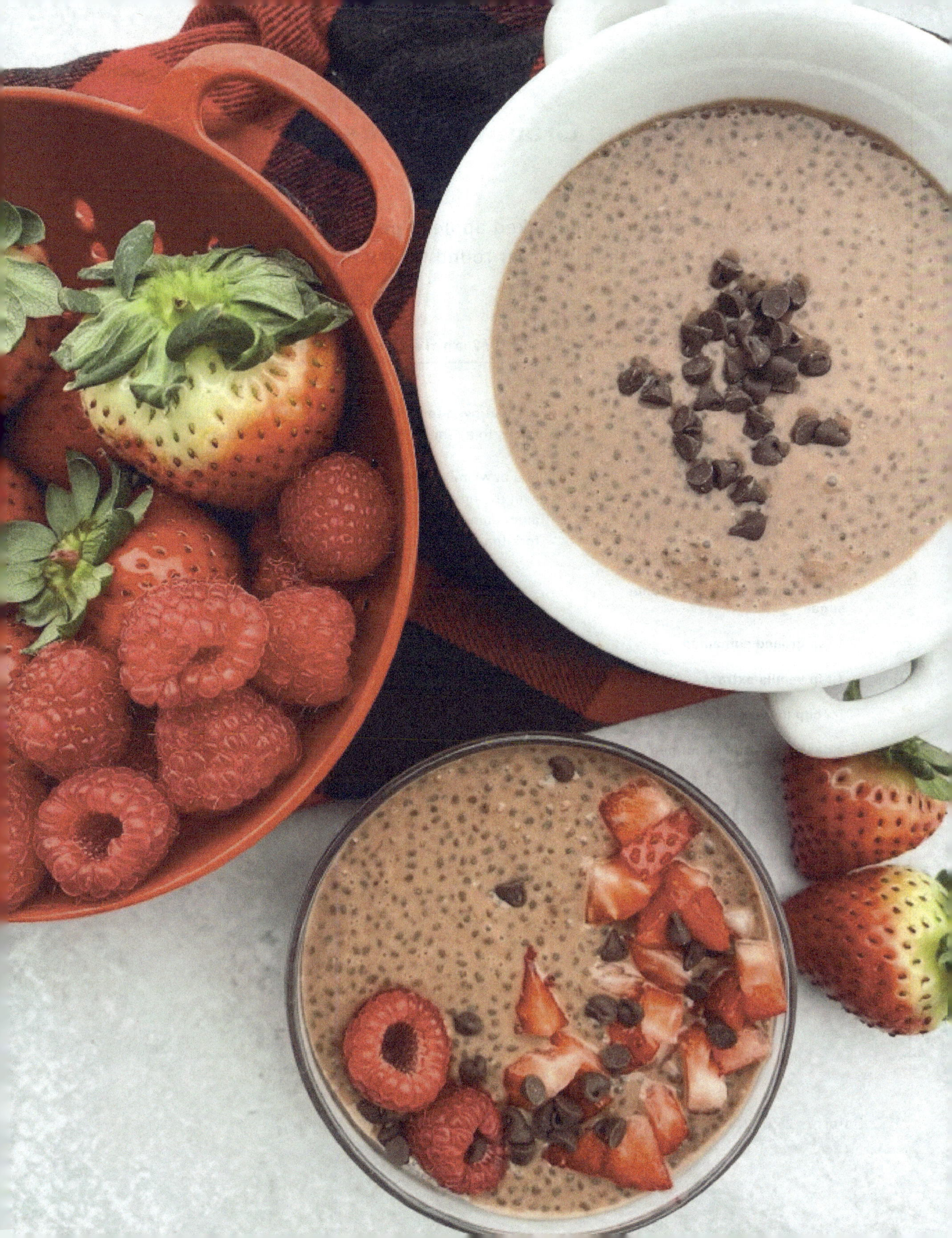

Orange Cranberry Baked Apples

Warm and comforting, this baked apple is perfect for breakfast or dessert. Make them all year round for a satisfying treat!

SERVES 8, 1/2 apple per serving

4 medium apples, core removed

2 cups of water

2 cinnamon sticks

Filling

2 tbsp melted butter of choice

2 tbsp brown sugar or coconut sugar

1 tsp ground cinnamon

1 tsp vanilla extract

¼ cup unsweetened applesauce

2 dashes of ground nutmeg

Zest and juice of one small orange

⅓ cup chopped dried cranberries

⅓ cup chopped pecans

¼ cup old-fashioned oats

Pinch of salt

Preheat oven to 375 degrees. Add the water and cinnamon sticks to a 2-quart or larger Dutch oven or deep casserole dish.

In a bowl, mix together all the filling ingredients. Fill each apple with the mixture and place in the Dutch oven. Cover with lid or aluminum foil and bake for 30–40 minutes or until apples are fork-tender. Serve warm with Greek yogurt or ice cream.

PRODUCT TIP

The best apples for this recipe are Honey Crisp, Pink Lady, Gala, or Jonagold. Feel free to try a tart apple like a Granny Smith.

Calories 170 | Carbs 22g | Fat 5g | Protein 3g | Fiber 4g | Sodium 30mg

Hash Brown Waffles

When I first created this recipe, I was making it almost daily. These are great for a special brunch menu or just a quick breakfast. You can switch up the seasoning to whatever you like with potatoes!

SERVES 4, 1 waffle per serving

1 cup frozen hash browns, warmed slightly in the microwave

1/2 tbsp softened butter of choice

1/2 tbsp neutral oil

1/2 slice of dairy-free or regular cheddar cheese, cut into small pieces

1/8 tsp seasoned salt of choice

Mix everything together in a bowl. Preheat a mini waffle maker and once hot, place 1/3 cup of the mixture in the waffle maker and close the lid.

After the light turns off, cook for another 3–4 minutes to cook through and make crispy.

Remove the waffle with a fork and repeat until all of the mixture is cooked.

COOKING TIP

I use a mini waffle maker for this recipe, but you can use a bigger size and section them off into individual waffles. Make sure to allow enough time, past the normal waffle cook time, to get crispy; otherwise, they will be soft and not cooked through.

Calories 87 | Carbs 6g | Fat 6g | Protein 0g | Fiber 1g | Sodium 60mg

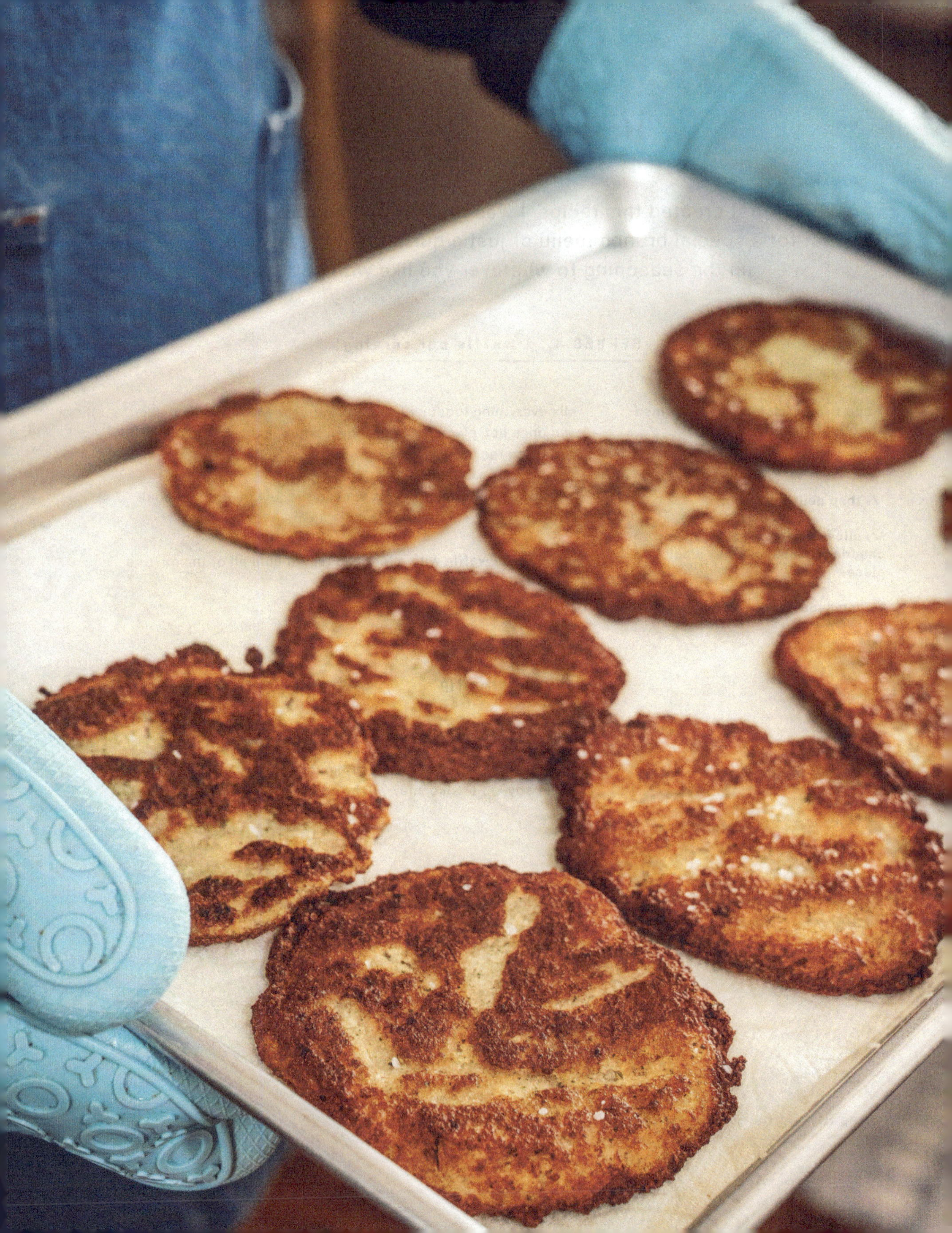

Creamy Style Potato Pancakes

Here is a taste of my childhood. I grew up in a Jewish-American home eating potato pancakes with applesauce or sour cream. They are hands down my favorite. Kids will love this tasty alternative to hash browns.

SERVES 4, 3 pancakes per serving

1 lb russet potatoes, peeled and cut in chunks

1 small, sweet onion, peeled and cut in chunks

2 stalks of celery, cut in chunks

1 tsp celery salt

1/2 tsp onion powder

1/2 tsp garlic powder

1/2 tsp dried parsley

Salt and pepper to taste

1 egg, beaten

1/3 cup plus 2 tbsp all-purpose gluten-free or regular flour

Neutral oil to fry, about 1/4 cup

Add the vegetables to a food processor and blend until very fine and mostly smooth.

Add the celery salt, onion powder, garlic powder, dried parsley, salt, pepper, egg, and flour and blend again.

Coat the bottom of a skillet with 1/4 cup of oil and set to medium heat.

Once hot, carefully add 1/4 cup of the mixture for each pancake and flatten it into 1/2-inch-thick rounds. Leave some space between each; I normally can cook 4 - 5 pancakes at a time in a larger skillet.

Cook each side for 3–4 minutes. Then place on paper towels to absorb extra oil. Repeat this step until all of the batter is used. Salt the tops and serve with applesauce or sour cream.

COOKING TIPS

The egg can be omitted or a flax egg (1 tablespoon of ground flaxseed + 3 tablespoons of water) can be used, but the pancakes will be more delicate to flip.

You can substitute gluten-free all-purpose flour, which will not affect the texture.

Sisters Apple Sauce recipe on page 27...

Calories 205 | Carbs 22g | Fat 11g | Protein 4g | Fiber 2g | Sodium 150mg

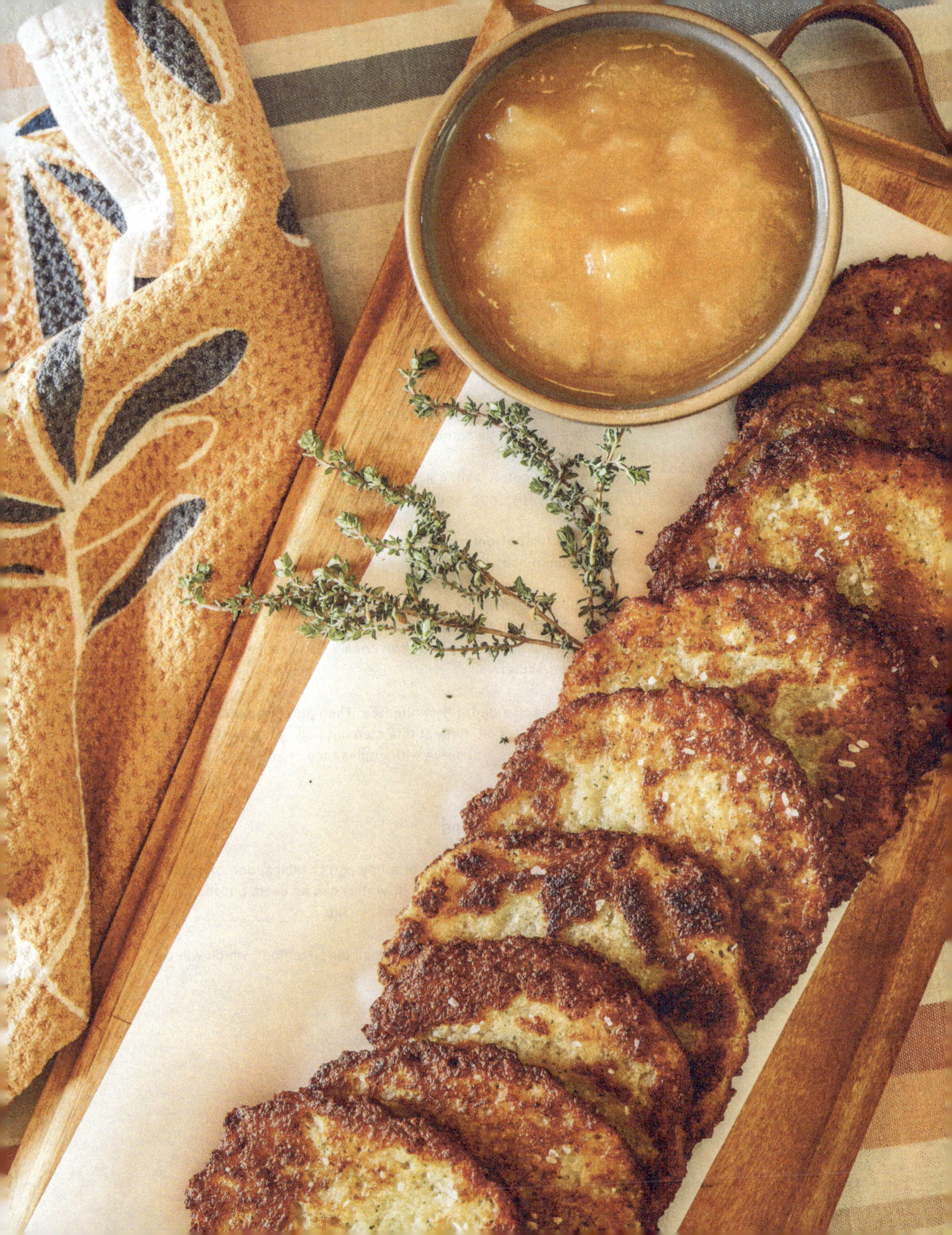

Sisters Apple Sauce

This super simple applesauce pairs perfectly with the **Creamy Style Potato Pancakes** (page 25). Use on top of the pancakes or on the side.

SERVES 16, 1/4 cup per serving

5 lbs mix of red and green apples, peeled, cored and cut into chunks

1 cup water

2 tbsp brown or coconut sugar

2 tsp fresh lemon juice

Add all the ingredients to an electric pressure cooker. Cook on high pressure for 8 minutes, then manually release the pressure.

Use an immersion blender to puree to your desired consistency. Cool, then serve or store in refrigerator.

PRODUCT TIP

I love the variety of apples we grow in my region. There are so many options! Choose a variety of cooking apples, some sweet and some tart. You can learn more online about which apples are best for cooking in your area.

Calories 79 | Carbs 21g | Fat 0g | Protein 0g | Fiber 4g | Sodium 2mg

Strawberry Smoothie Muffins

Want your kids to eat beets? We all know this can be a difficult vegetable to introduce to our families. But sneaking them into a sweet breakfast muffin might just do the trick!

MAKES 12 MUFFINS, 1 muffin per serving

8 oz frozen strawberries, defrosted and drained of juice

2.5 oz or 2 - 3 small canned beets in water, drained and rinsed

1 large banana, peeled and broken in chunks

1/3 cup dairy-free or regular vanilla yogurt

2 tsp pure vanilla extract

2 large eggs

1/4 cup neutral oil

1/4 cup white granulated sugar or coconut sugar

2 tsp baking powder

3/4 tsp salt

1/2 tsp baking soda

1 1/2 cups all-purpose gluten-free or regular flour

1/2 cup old-fashioned oats

1 cup diced fresh strawberries

1 tsp all-purpose flour

Topping Option

1 tsp strawberry jam on each muffin

Preheat the oven to 375 degrees and line a muffin pan with liners or use a silicone muffin pan.

To a blender or food processor, add the defrosted strawberries, beets, banana, yogurt, and vanilla extract. Blend until smooth and set aside.

To a medium mixing bowl, add the eggs, oil, and sugar and whisk well. Add the fruit mixture, baking powder, salt, and baking soda and whisk until well combined.

Add flour and oats to a separate small bowl and stir together. Add the flour to the wet mixture and whisk again until batter is just combined, do not over-mix. In a small bowl, toss together the fresh strawberries and flour. Add strawberries to the batter and toss until distributed. Allow batter to sit for 10 minutes.

Divide batter evenly into 12 muffin cups, 3/4 full, and top each with 1 teaspoon of jam, if using. Bake for 22–24 minutes or until a toothpick comes out clean. Start checking the muffins at 20 minutes. Remove from oven and let cool. Freeze or refrigerate until ready to eat.

COOKING TIP

Using a scale is the best way to ensure correct measurements of the strawberries and beets. Make sure to blend the fruit and beets until very smooth and no pieces are present.

Calories 167 | Carbs 20g | Fat 8g | Protein 4g | Fiber 3g | Sodium 98mg

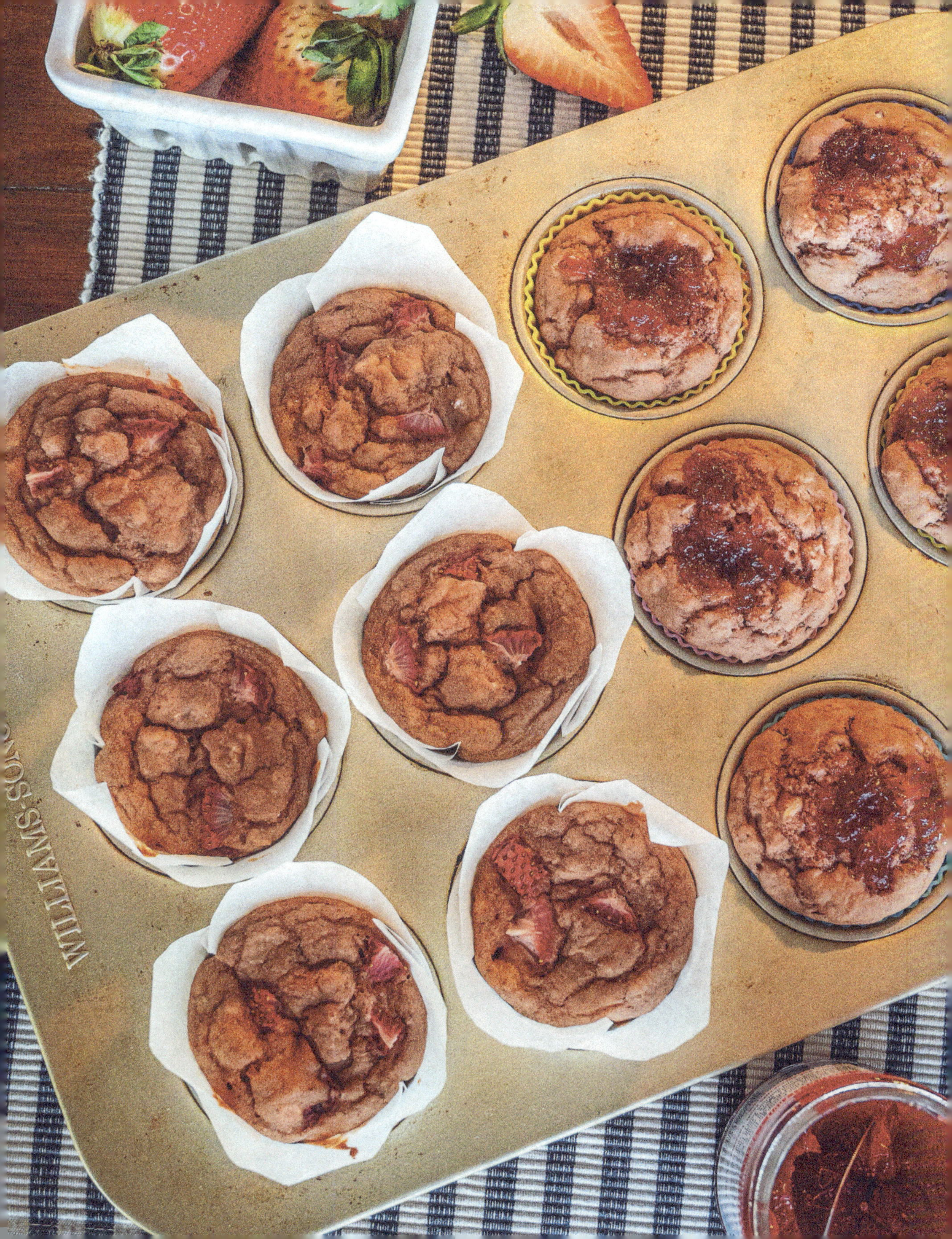
WILLIAMS-SON

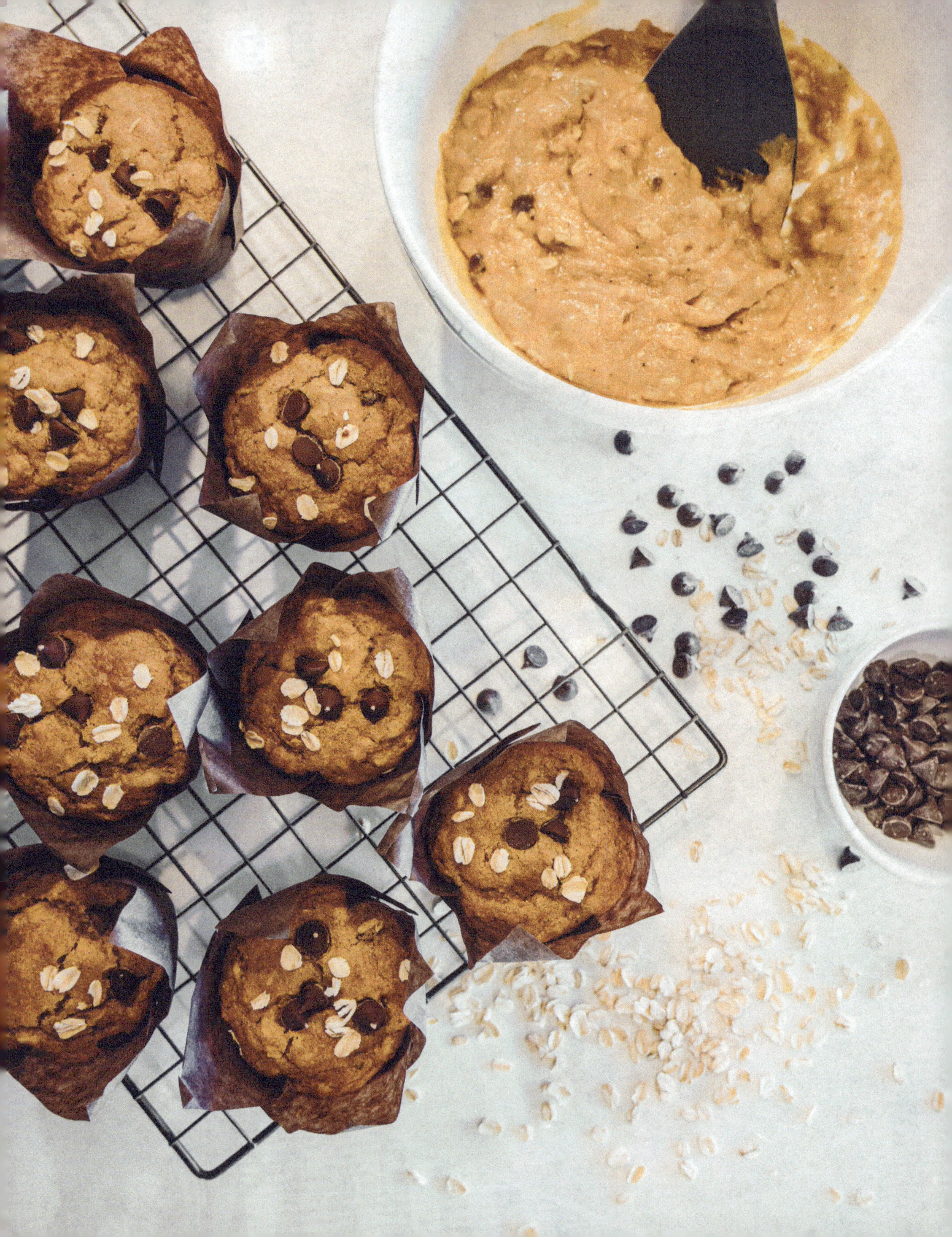

Pumpkin Chocolate Oat Muffins

By far our family's favorite muffin! The flavor of the pumpkin is not too strong and works well with the chocolate for a not-too-sweet breakfast muffin. Pumpkin is not just for fall; make these any time of year. You'll be happy you did!

MAKES 12 MUFFINS, 1 muffin per serving

½ cup pumpkin puree

2 large eggs or 2 vegan replacement eggs

⅓ cup neutral oil or melted butter of choice

⅔ cup maple syrup

1 tsp vanilla extract

1 cup all-purpose gluten-free or regular flour

¼ cup almond flour

½ cup old-fashioned rolled oats, plus more for topping

1 ½ tsp pumpkin pie spice

2 tsp baking powder

½ tsp baking soda

½ tsp salt

⅓ cup semi-sweet chocolate chips

Topping Options

Pumpkin seeds, rolled oats, or chopped nuts

Preheat oven to 350 degrees. Line muffin tins with muffin liners or use a silicone muffin pan.

Add the pumpkin puree, eggs, oil, maple syrup, and vanilla to a bowl and whisk together well.

Add both flours, oats, pumpkin pie spice, baking powder, baking soda, and salt to the wet ingredients and whisk together until just combined. Fold in the chocolate chips.

Divide batter evenly into 12 muffin cups, about ¾ full, and sprinkle each with topping options. Bake for 20–22 minutes or until toothpick comes out clean and top feels set.

COOKING TIP

Cook time will vary depending on the size of the muffin tin and how full it is. Adjust cook time accordingly.

Calories 166 | Carbs 19g | Fat 9g | Protein 3g | Fiber 2g | Sodium 50mg

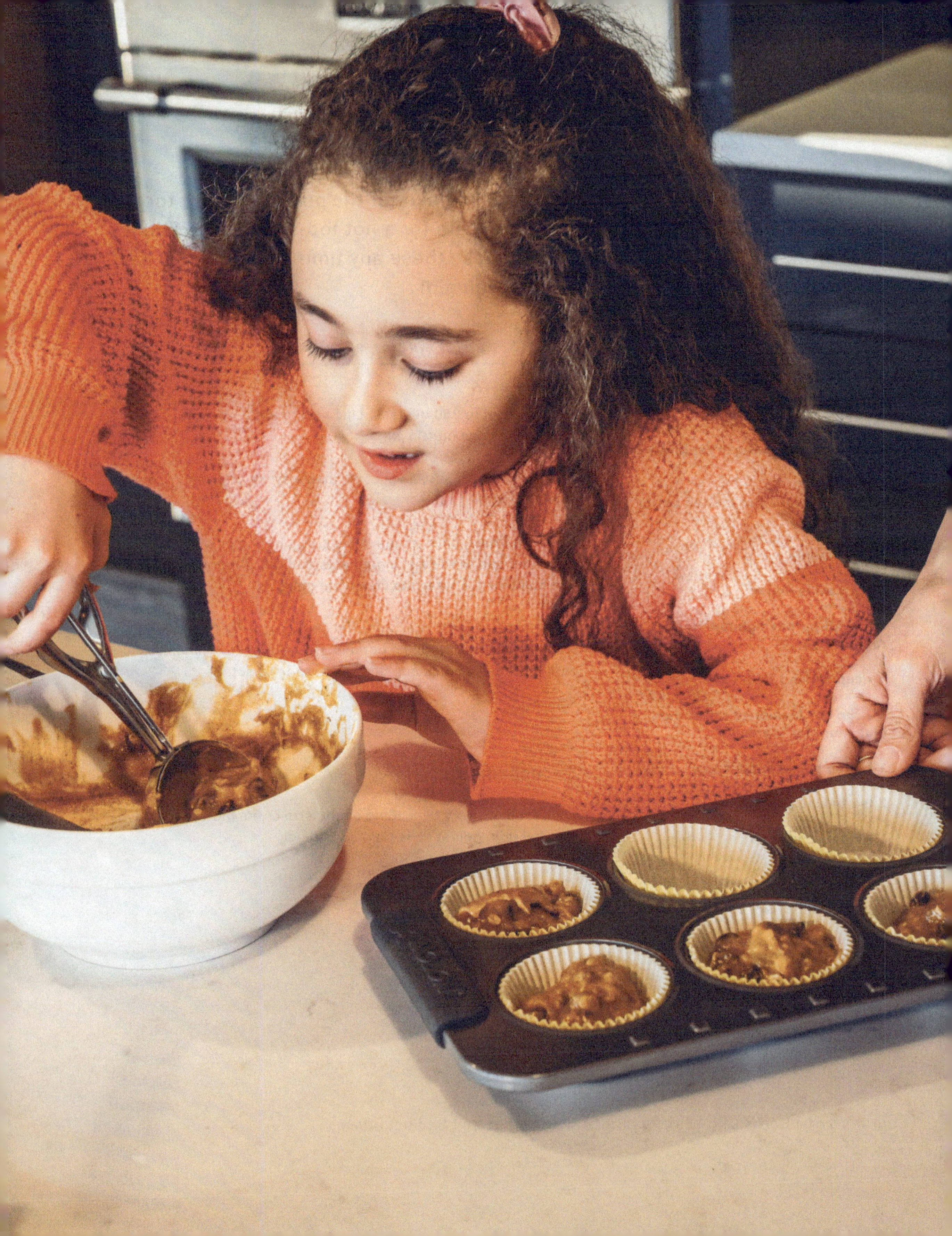

Double Chocolate Zucchini Muffins

Okay, I know I said the Pumpkin Chocolate Chip muffins were our family's favorite, but these are right up there! Double Chocolate Zucchini Muffins are so close to a mini cake, you could serve them as a dessert. Sweetened with maple syrup, for a healthier sugar alternative, your family will enjoy any time of day.

MAKES 12 MUFFINS, 1 muffin per serving

1 cup almond flour

1 cup all-purpose gluten-free or regular flour

½ cup unsweetened cocoa powder

½ tsp baking soda

2 tsp baking powder

½ tsp salt

¾ cup pure maple syrup

2 eggs or 2 vegan replacement eggs

½ cup melted coconut oil or butter of choice, cooled slightly

¼ cup unsweetened applesauce

½ tbsp instant dried decaf coffee, optional

1 tbsp pure vanilla extract

1 cup finely shredded zucchini, squeezed of extra water with a towel

¾ cup semi-sweet or dark chocolate chips

Preheat oven to 350 degrees and line a muffin tin with liners.

Add the almond flour, all-purpose flour, cocoa powder, baking soda, baking powder, and salt to a mixing bowl. Whisk together and set aside.

In a larger bowl, combine the maple syrup, eggs, melted oil or butter, applesauce, instant coffee, and vanilla extract. Whisk together; then add the shredded zucchini.

Add the dry ingredients to the wet and fold together until just combined. Fold in the chocolate chips; don't overmix.

Divide into 12 muffin cups and bake for 22–24 minutes or until toothpick comes out clean and top feels set. Cool in muffin pan for 10 minutes, then serve.

Calories 262 | Carbs 31g | Fat 14g | Protein 3g | Fiber 2g | Sodium 322mg

Green Protein Smoothie

Want your family to eat more greens? I understand how hard that can be. Bring on the green smoothies! They won't taste the spinach at all!

SERVES 2, 1/2 of the recipe per serving

- ¾ - 1 cup unsweetened dairy-free or regular milk
- 1 small green apple, core removed and cut into chunks
- 2 cups packed baby spinach
- 1 cup ice
- 1 tbsp chia seeds
- 1 tbsp almond or peanut butter
- 3 tbsp vanilla protein powder or ½ scoop
- 1 medium banana
- 1 tsp honey or agave, optional

Add all the ingredients to a blender and blend until very smooth. Divide into two cups and serve.

🛒 PRODUCT TIP

My two favorite plant-based proteins are Vanilla Orgain and Vega brands. Find them at most grocery stores or online.

Calories 257 | Carbs 36g | Fat 8g | Protein 13g | Fiber 9g | Sodium 133mg

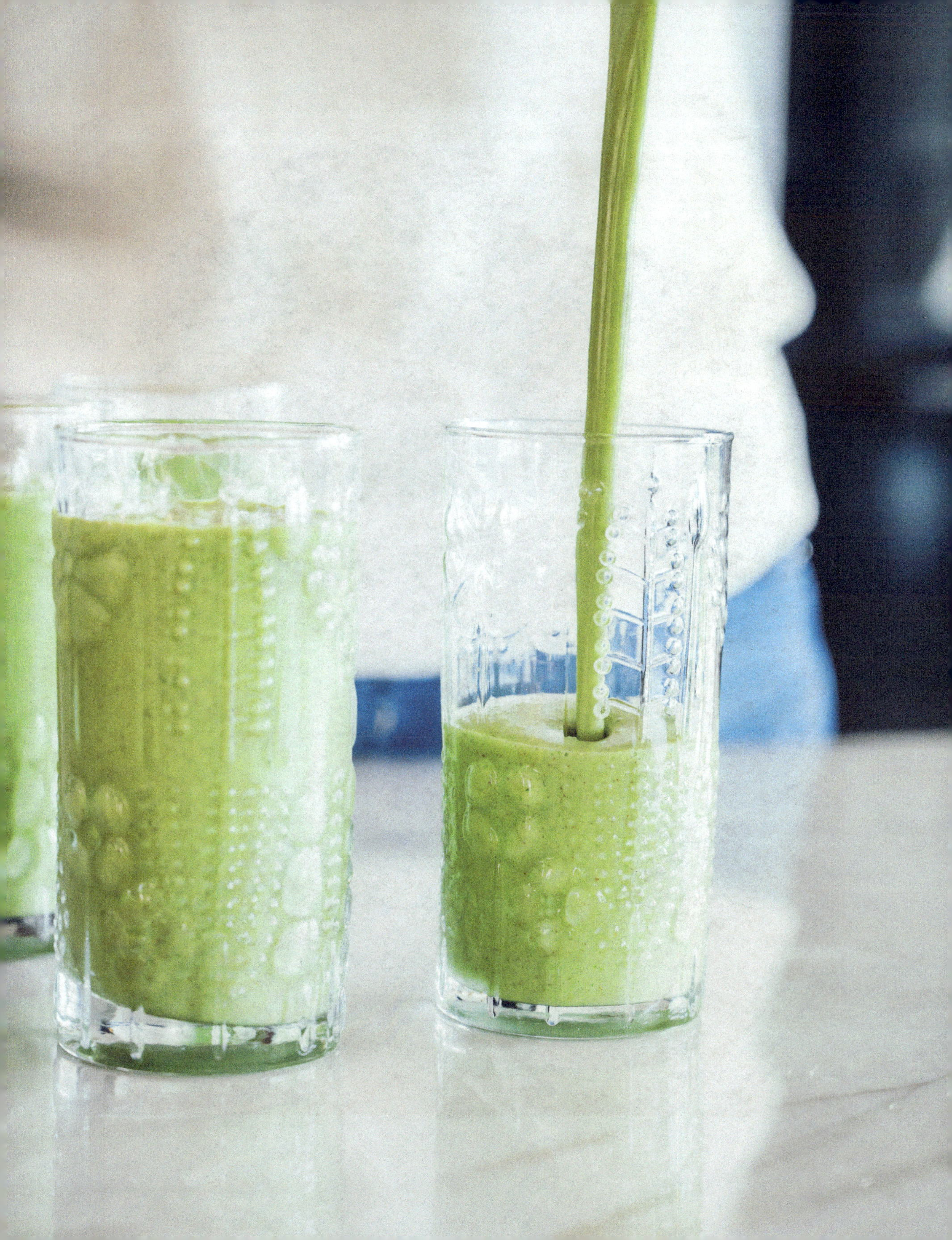

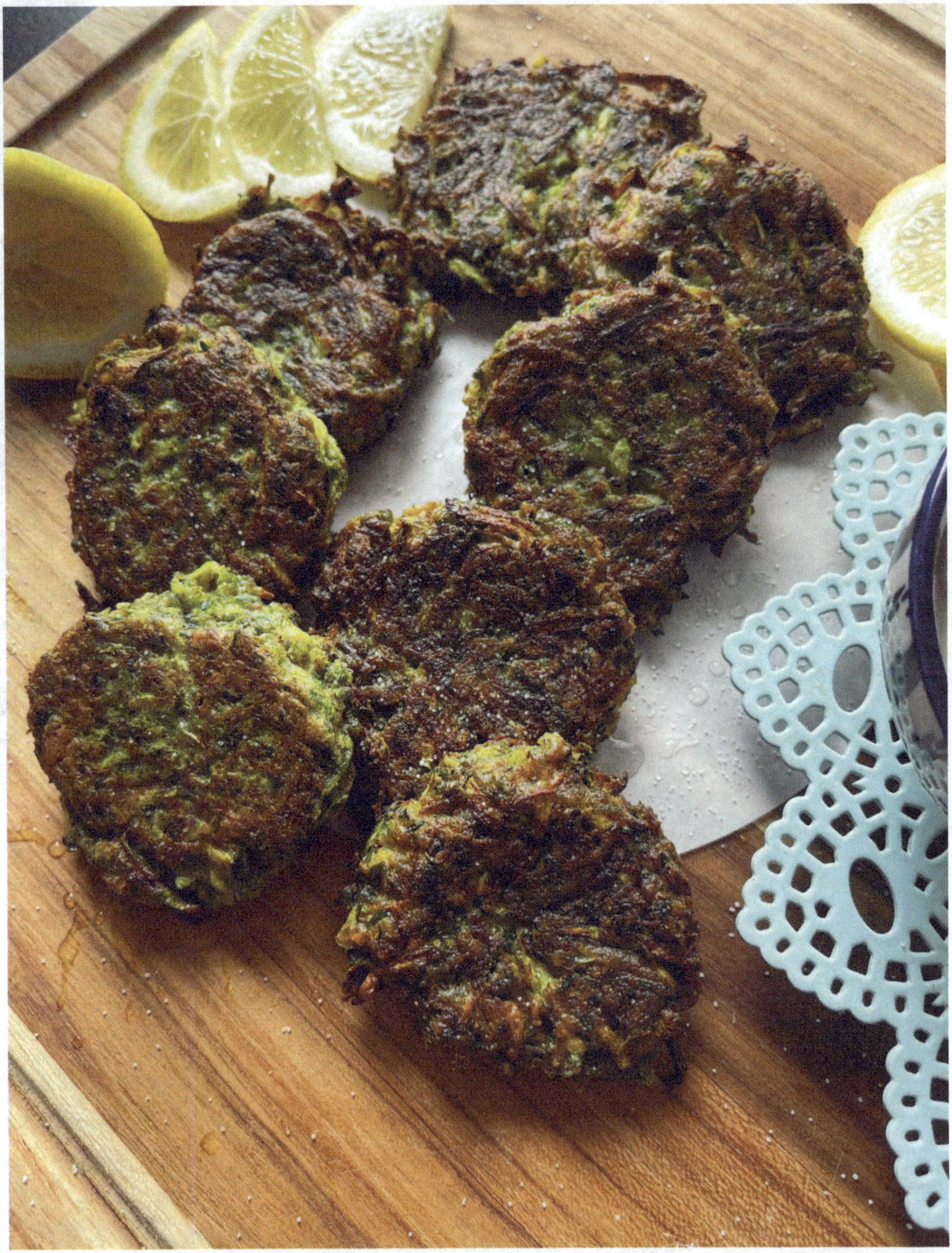

Green Veggie Pancakes

These savory pancakes might be green, but they are delicious! On top of that, they are super healthy and loaded with everything good for you!

SERVES 4, 2 pancakes per serving

1 tbsp ground flaxseed + 2 tbsp water or 1 egg

1 cup coarsely chopped and packed curly kale

¼ cup chopped green onion

¼ cup chopped cilantro

2 cloves fresh garlic, minced

1 small zucchini, stem ends removed

½ tsp ground turmeric

½ tsp baking powder

¼ cup all-purpose gluten-free or regular flour

2 tbsp arrowroot, corn, or potato starch

¼ cup nutritional yeast

1 tbsp water

Salt and pepper, to taste

2 - 3 tbsp neutral oil

In a small bowl, mix the flaxseed and water and set aside to thicken. If using an egg, add it to the bowl and whisk.

Add the kale, green onion, cilantro, and garlic to a food processor and pulse until finely chopped. Remove the blade and replace with the shredding attachment. Shred the zucchini, then transfer the veggies into a medium bowl.

Add the egg, turmeric, baking powder, flour, starch, nutritional yeast, and water to the bowl with the veggies and mix. Season with salt and pepper. Allow the mixture to sit for 5 minutes while pan is heating up.

Heat a skillet to medium heat and coat the bottom with a thin layer of oil, about 1 - 2 tablespoons. Once hot, use a 1 ½ - 2-inch cookie scoop to measure the batter, spreading each pancake to an even thickness. Do not overcrowd the pan.

Fry on each side for 3–4 minutes or until golden and drain on paper towel. Repeat batches and add more oil when needed. Season with salt and serve!

🍲 COOKING TIP

Make sure your pan is not too hot; otherwise, the inside won't have enough time to cook before the outside gets dark. You don't need much oil either, just enough to coat the pan for each batch of pancakes.

Calories 152 | Carbs 10g | Fat 10g | Protein 6g | Fiber 4g | Sodium 160mg

CH 1

Bright Mornings

Chunky Monkey Granola

This granola recipe is a take on the popular flavor combination of banana, chocolate, and walnuts. The oat bran gives it an added boost of nutrition to start the day right.

SERVES 18, 1/3 cup per serving

- 2 ripe bananas, mashed
- 1/2 cup maple syrup
- 1/4 cup neutral oil
- 4 cups old-fashioned oats
- 1/2 cup oat or wheat bran
- 3/4 cup walnut or pecan pieces
- 3 tbsp unsweetened cocoa powder
- 1/4 tsp salt
- 1 tbsp pure vanilla extract
- 1/3 cup mini chocolate chips

In a large mixing bowl, add the mashed bananas, then add the rest of the ingredients except the chocolate chips. Toss all ingredients together well.

Preheat the oven to 300 degrees and line a baking sheet with parchment paper. Spread granola evenly on a baking sheet. Bake for 45 minutes for soft baked texture, stirring every 15 minutes. Bake for another 15 minutes for a dryer, crisp granola.

Add the chocolate chips when completely cooled. Store the granola in an air-tight container in the refrigerator for up to two weeks.

COOKING TIP

Make this granola recipe the night before and cool on the counter. In the morning stir in the chocolate chips and serve with your favorite yogurt.

Calories 166 | Carbs 25g | Fat 6g | Protein 4g | Fiber 3g | Sodium 2mg

Eggy Veggie Muffins

You might have tried egg muffins for breakfast. I love this recipe because it is loaded with veggies and whole grain brown rice, which makes them extra filling. Choose whatever vegetables your family likes!

MAKES 12 MUFFINS, 1 muffin per serving

2 tbsp neutral oil

1/2 red bell pepper, minced

1/2 white or red onion, minced

1/2 zucchini, minced

1 bottle (12 oz) of Just Egg or 8 large eggs

1 cup cooked brown rice, cooled

2 Roma tomatoes, seeds and liquid removed, then small diced

1/4 tsp garlic powder

1/4 tsp onion powder

1/8 tsp black pepper

1 tsp salt

3 tbsp finely chopped green onion

2 tbsp finely chopped fresh parsley

1/2 cup dairy-free or regular shredded mozzarella

Preheat the oven to 375 degrees and spray a muffin tin with cooking spray or use a silicone muffin mold and skip the spray.

In a medium skillet, add the oil, red bell pepper, onion, and zucchini and cook for 3–4 minutes until just fork-tender.

Meanwhile, add the Just Egg to a mixing bowl. If using eggs, whisk thoroughly before adding the other ingredients. Add the rice, tomatoes, garlic, and onion powder, black pepper, salt, green onion, parsley, and mozzarella to the egg bowl and mix until well combined.

Cool the cooked veggies slightly, then mix into the egg base. Divide into the muffin cups evenly. Bake for 20 minutes. Cool slightly then serve.

PRODUCT TIP

This recipe uses a product called Just Egg. It's relatively new to the market, but is available now at most grocery stores. It keeps these egg bites nice and moist even after being refrigerated for a while.

Calories 93 | Carbs 5g | Fat 6g | Protein 4g | Fiber 1g | Sodium 123mg

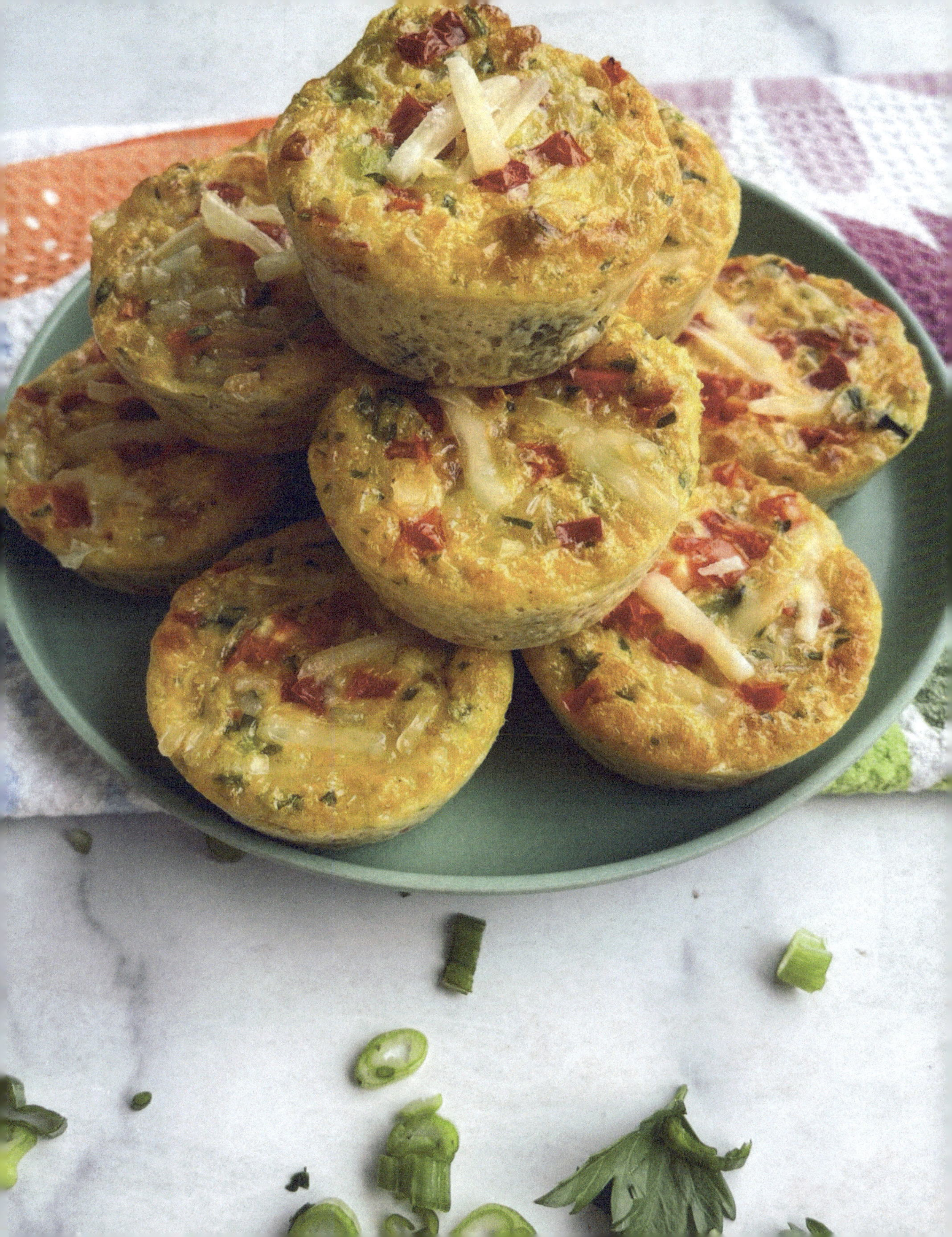

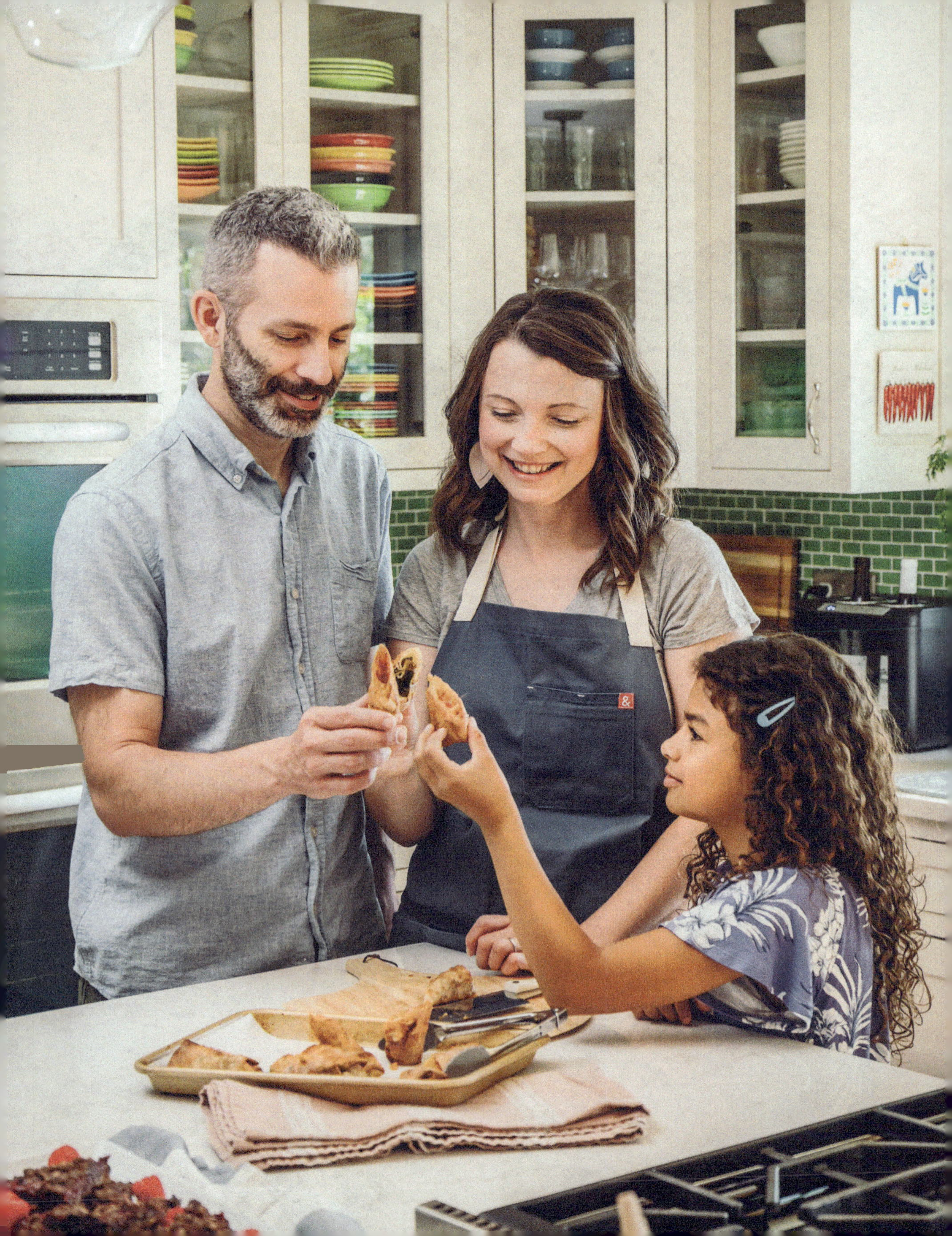

Snack Attack

Apple Cider Donuts	**45**
Protein Chocolate Chip Cookie Bars	**46**
Herb Feta Dip	**49**
Fluffy Cornbread Muffins	**51**
Almond Joy Energy Bites	**52**
Dark Chocolate Raspberry Oat Bars	**55**
Pizza Rolls	**56**
Chocolate Brownie Dip	**59**
Strawberry Rhubarb Sauce	**60**
Jalapeño Popper Dip	**61**
Pucker-Up Lemon Hummus	**63**

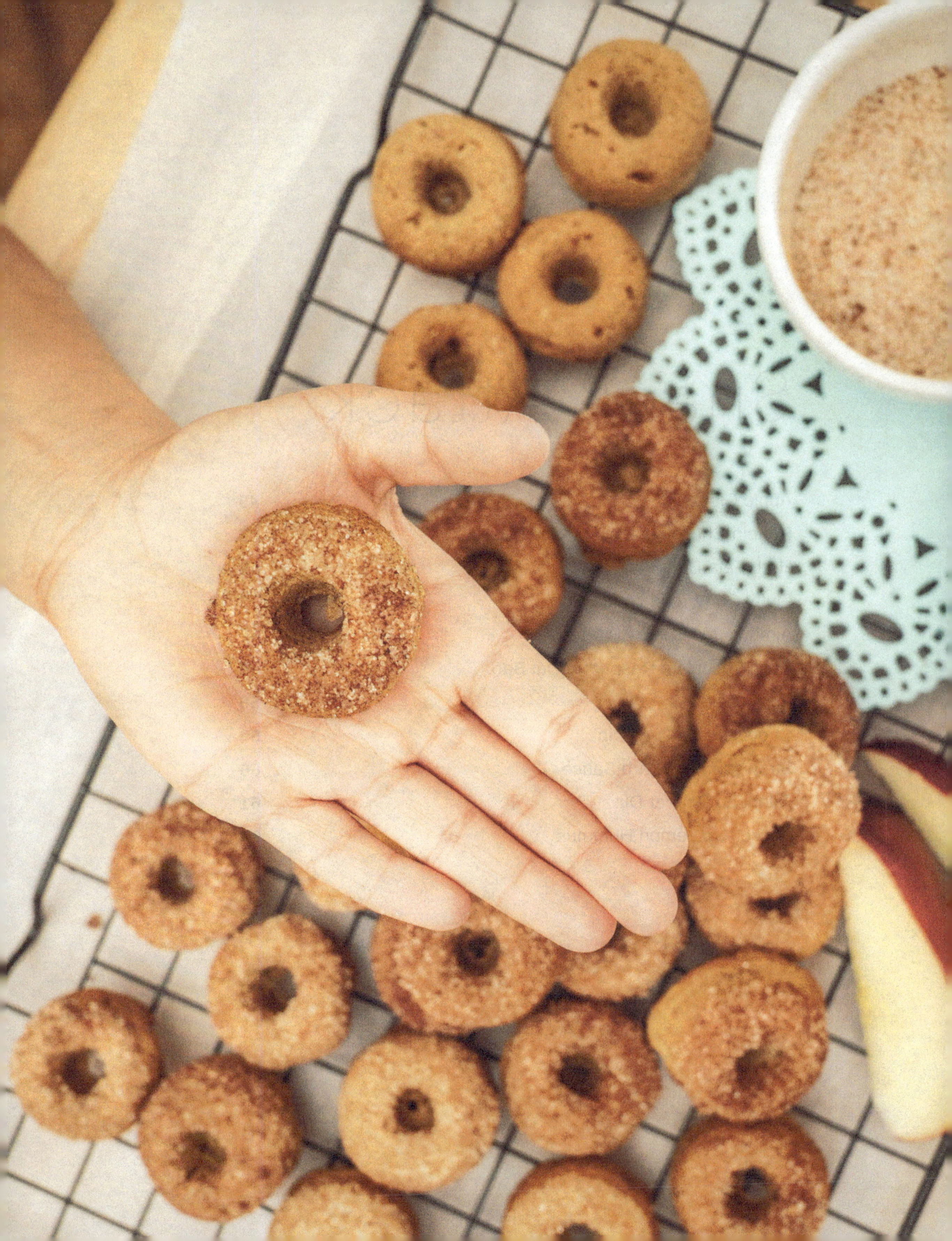

Apple Cider Donuts

These mini donuts are perfect for a pre- or post-game treat or after-school snack. They taste like fall has arrived, but really can be made all year round!

MAKES 36-38 MINI DONUTS, 1 donut per serving

1 ¼ cups all-purpose gluten-free or regular flour

¼ cup almond flour

2 tsp baking powder

½ tsp baking soda

½ tsp salt

⅓ cup coconut sugar or brown sugar

½ tbsp ground cinnamon

2 - 4 pinches or dashes of ground nutmeg

1 egg or 2 egg replacements*

1 tbsp vanilla extract

1 ½ tsp apple extract, optional

½ cup apple cider

½ cup apple butter or unsweetened applesauce

½ cup melted coconut oil or butter of choice

¾ cup minced or small diced sweet or tart baking apples, peeled

Toppings

⅓ cup melted coconut oil or butter of choice

1 tbsp ground cinnamon

¼ cup white, coconut, or brown sugar

Preheat the oven to 350 degrees and spray a mini donut pan with cooking spray.

Add both flours, baking powder, baking soda, salt, coconut sugar, cinnamon, and nutmeg to a large bowl and whisk together. Set aside.

In a blender, add the egg or egg replacement, extracts, cider, and apple butter to the blender and blend until smooth. While the blender is running, slowly pour in the coconut oil. Add the wet ingredients to the dry and mix together. Fold in the apples.

Transfer batter to a pastry bag or plastic bag and cut off the tip. Fill each donut well halfway with batter. Bake for 10–12 minutes. Repeat until all batter is used, spraying pan with cooking spray for each additional batch.

Remove from oven and tap out onto a cooling rack. Allow to cool for 10–15 minutes or longer, if possible.

Add the coconut oil to one bowl and the cinnamon, sugar, and nutmeg to another bowl. Dip the tops of the donuts in the oil, shake off excess, then dip into the cinnamon sugar. Store leftovers at room temperature in an airtight container or freeze for later.

🛒 PRODUCT TIP

*I have found Neat Egg to be the best vegan egg replacement, especially for donuts. Many grocery stores are now carrying it and it is available online.

Calories 88 | Carbs 10g | Fat 6g | Protein 0g | Fiber 0g | Sodium 39mg

Protein Chocolate Chip Cookie Bars

You'll be amazed by the flavor of these bars. Soft, chocolatey, and slightly sweet, your family won't sacrifice any cookie satisfaction with these!

SERVES 15, 1 bar per serving

1 stick or 8 tbsp unsalted butter, softened, can use dairy-free option

1 cup coconut sugar or brown sugar

2 eggs

½ cup smooth peanut butter

2 tsp vanilla extract

½ cup vanilla protein powder

1 tsp baking soda

¼ tsp salt

1 ½ cups all-purpose gluten-free or regular flour

1 cup semi-sweet chocolate chips

Preheat the oven to 350 degrees. Line a 9x13 baking dish with aluminum foil or parchment paper and coat with cooking spray. Set aside.

In a large mixing bowl, cream together the butter and coconut sugar for 1–2 minutes using a hand mixer or stand mixer.

Add the eggs, peanut butter, vanilla, protein powder, baking soda, and salt and cream again until mixture is smooth, pale, and fluffy.

Add the flour and mix until just combined. Fold in the chocolate chips.

Spread the dough evenly in the lined baking dish and smooth out the top. Bake for 16–18 minutes; a toothpick should come out clean and edges will be slightly browned. Cool for 30 minutes before removing bars and cutting. Freeze or store in the refrigerator.

PRODUCT TIP

My two favorite plant-based proteins are Vanilla Orgain and Vega brands. Find them at most grocery stores or online.

Calories 287 | Carbs 34g | Fat 15g | Protein 7g | Fiber 2g | Sodium 116mg

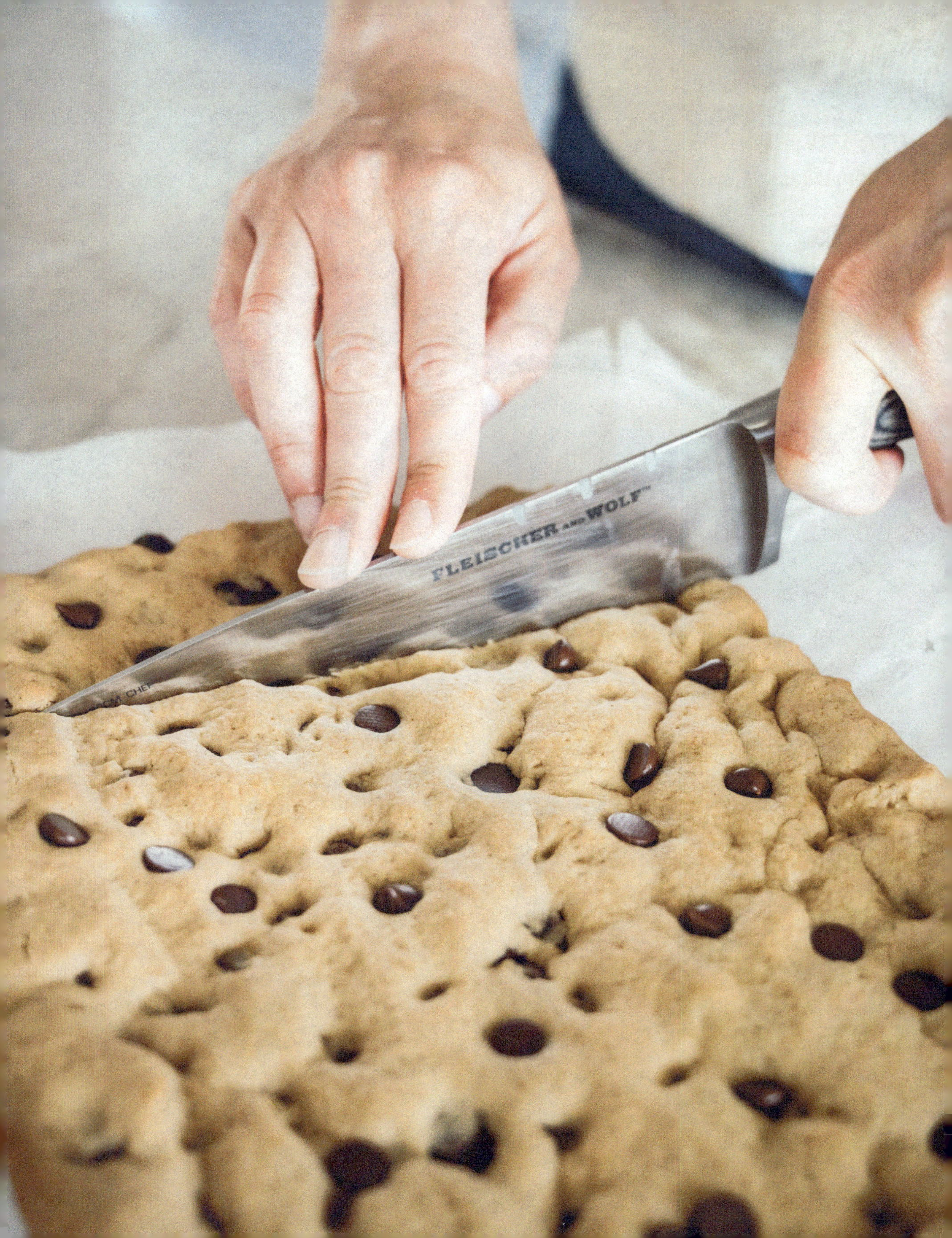
FLEISCHER AND WOLF

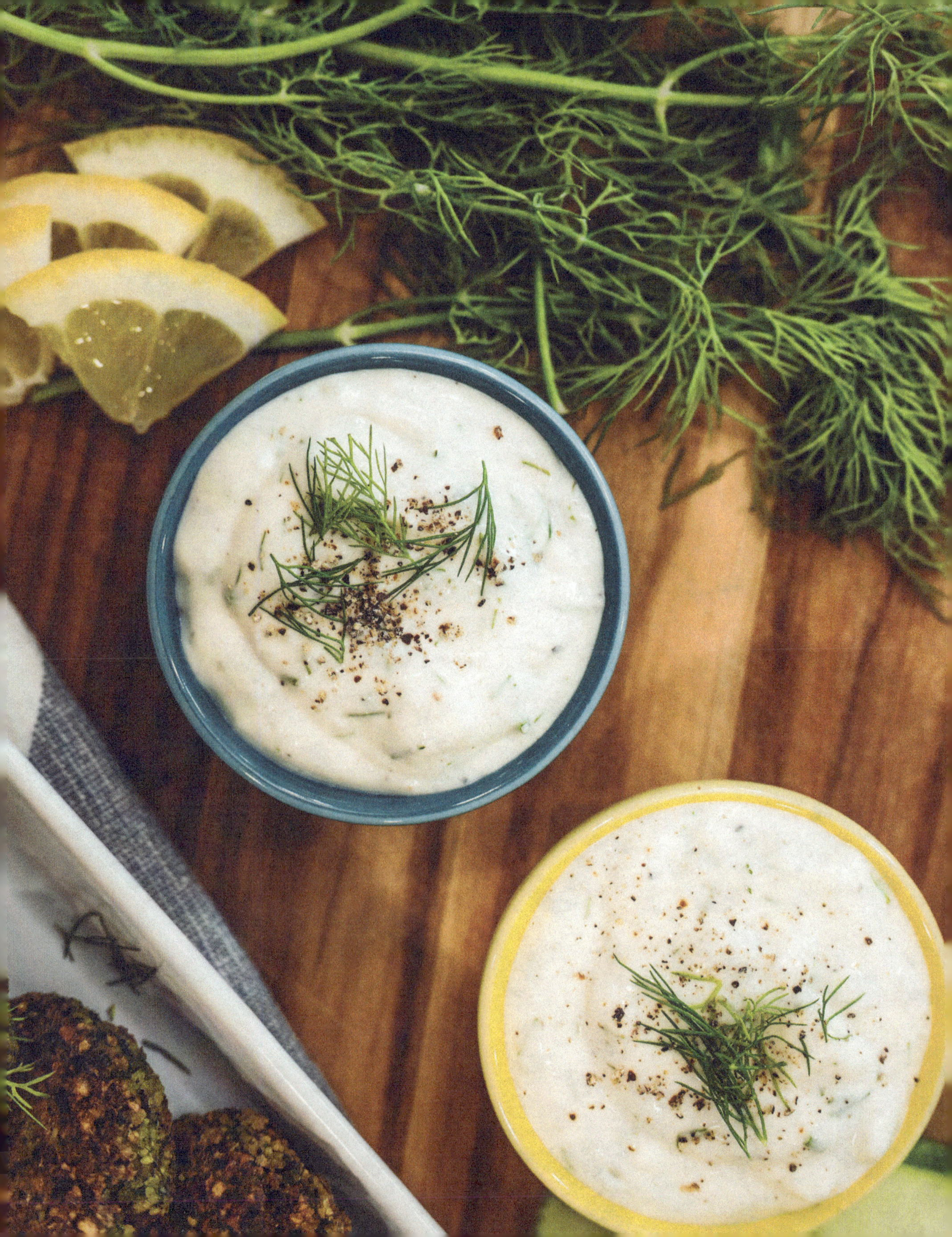

Herb Feta Dip

This dip is a delicious alternative to **Tzatziki Sauce** (page 146). You can use it to dress up any protein or as a dip for pita bread. It also makes a great salad dressing.

SERVES 6, 3 tbsp per serving

4 oz dairy-free or regular feta cheese crumbles

¼ cup dairy-free or regular sour cream

½ cup plain yogurt or mayonnaise of choice

2 tbsp fresh lemon juice

2 - 3 tbsp of water to thin

¼ cup fresh parsley, finely chopped

1 tbsp fresh dill or 1 tsp dried

Lots of coarse ground black pepper

Topping Option
Extra virgin olive oil drizzle

Add the feta, sour cream, yogurt or mayonnaise, lemon juice, and water to a food processor and blend until feta is crumbled and in small bits.

Transfer mixture to a bowl and stir in the parsley, dill, and pepper to taste. Mix together well. Taste for seasoning and drizzle with olive oil, if using.

MODIFICATION TIP

You can use a low-fat option for the sour cream, feta, and yogurt. The whole recipe can also be made dairy-free.

Calories 135 | Carbs 6g | Fat 11g | Protein 1g | Fiber 0g | Sodium 346mg

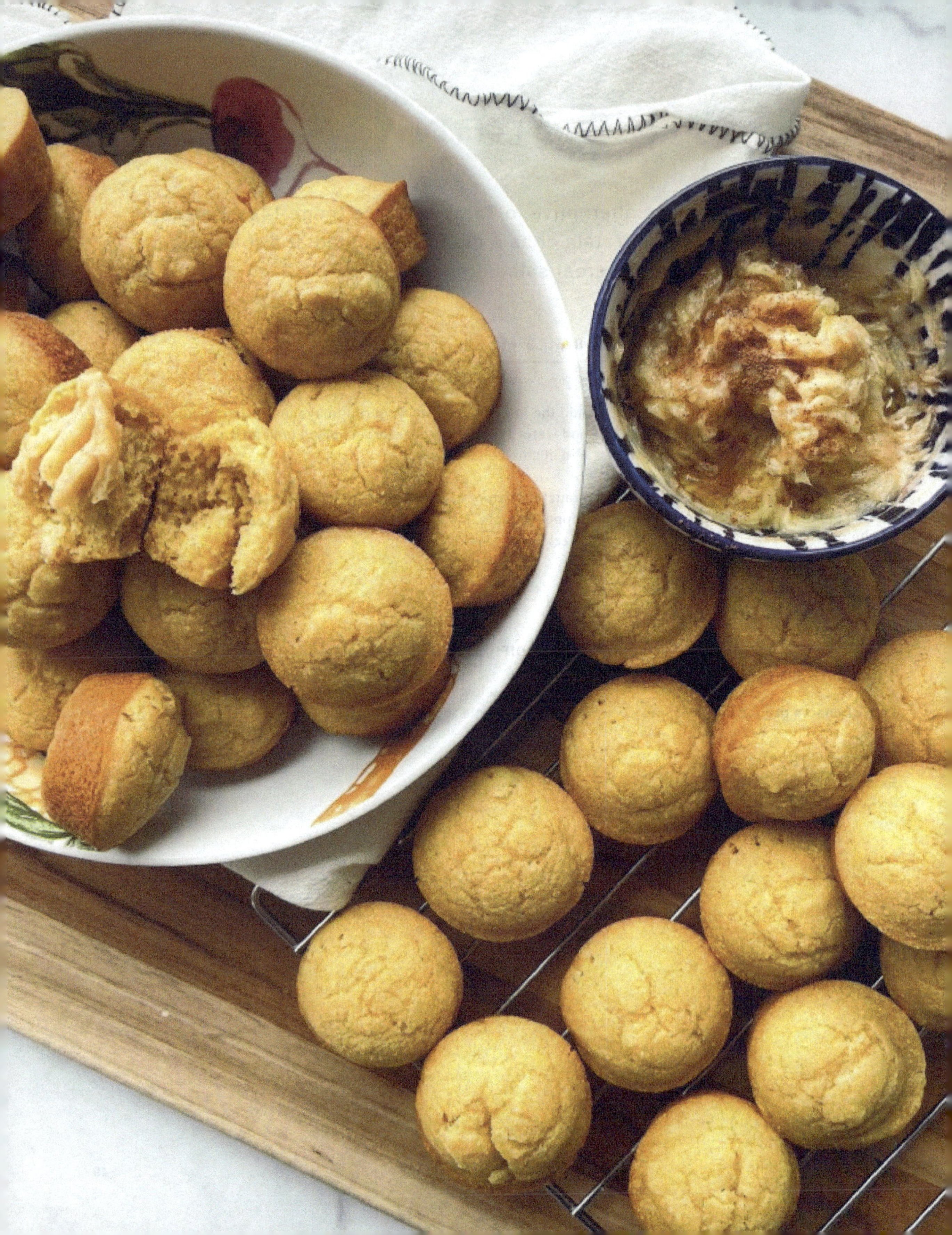

Fluffy Cornbread Muffins

These are fun little treats to be served as a snack or a side to chili or soup. They are also delicious for breakfast. Store them in the refrigerator for up to five days. Warm in the microwave and they are ready to enjoy!

MAKES 46-48 MINI OR 12 REGULAR SIZE MUFFINS

1 cup dairy-free or regular plain yogurt

¾ cup unsweetened plain dairy-free or regular milk*

1 tsp baking soda

¼ cup neutral oil

3 tbsp melted butter of choice

¼ cup honey or maple syrup

2 eggs or egg replacements

1 ½ cups yellow cornmeal

¾ cup all-purpose gluten-free or regular flour

2 tsp baking powder

1 tsp salt

Preheat oven to 350 degrees and spray a mini or regular-size muffin pan with cooking spray. If doing minis, you will need to spray the pan in between batches.

In a bowl, whisk together the yogurt, milk, and baking soda. This step will create a buttermilk for the cornbread. Set aside for 10 minutes.

In a large mixing bowl, whisk together the oil, butter, and honey; then add the eggs and whisk again.

Add the cornmeal, flour, baking powder, and salt to the large mixing bowl along with the yogurt mixture. Stir until combined; do not over mix. For best results, let batter rest for 5-10 minutes before scooping into muffin tin. This will help the cornmeal absorb the liquid and make the batter thicker and fluffier. Fill each muffin cup ¾ full with batter.

Bake the minis for 8-10 minutes or regular size for 22-24 minutes or until a toothpick comes out clean. Transfer to a cooling rack. Spray the muffin tin again, then repeat until all the batter is baked.

PRODUCT TIP

*I like oat, almond, or soy milk for a dairy-free option.

MODIFICATION TIP

For more of a flavor punch, add shredded cheddar, green onion, garlic powder, and/or minced jalapenos. You can make half plain and half for more adventurous eaters.

Per mini muffin   Calories 48 | Carbs 5g | Fat 3g | Protein 1g | Fiber 1g | Sodium 55mg
Per full size muffin Calories 182 | Carbs 20g | Fat 10g | Protein 4g | Fiber 2g | Sodium 220mg

Almond Joy Energy Bites

These energy bites are a great way to power up your kids before or after an activity. A food processor works best as the dates are very sticky. This is a fun one for kids to help make.

MAKES 25, 1 energy bite per serving

2 cups fresh Medjool dates, pitted

1/4 cup unsweetened cocoa powder

1 cup slivered or sliced almonds

2 - 3 tbsp unsweetened dairy-free milk

1/4 cup mini chocolate chips

1/2 cup finely shredded unsweetened coconut

Cooking spray

In a food processor, combine dates, cocoa powder, almonds, and 2 tablespoons of almond milk until it forms a ball and looks like a chunky paste. If dates are dry, add the other 1 tablespoon of milk.

Remove from processor and place mixture in bowl. Mix in the chocolate chips.

Using a small cookie scoop or spoon sprayed with cooking spray, form into 1-inch balls with hands. Roll each in shredded coconut to cover the outside. The bites can be refrigerated or frozen.

MODIFICATION TIP

If you don't like shredded coconut, you can eliminate or roll each bite in unsweetened cocoa powder.

Calories 75 | Carbs 12g | Fat 5g | Protein 4g | Fiber 3g | Sodium 10mg

Dark Chocolate Raspberry Oat Bars (page 55)

Snack Attack — CH 2

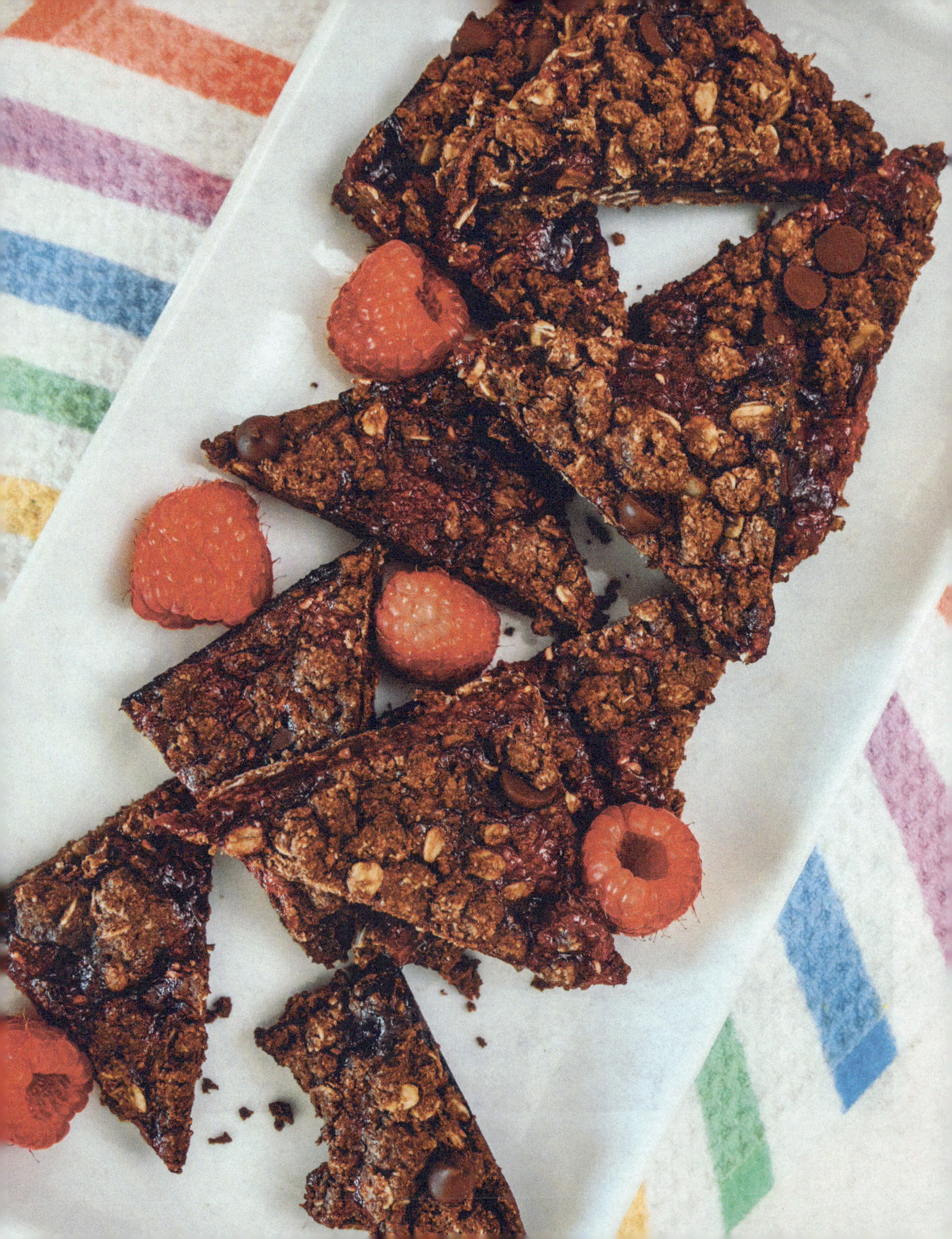

Dark Chocolate Raspberry Oat Bars

I've made this recipe for so many summer gatherings. You can certainly make it any time of the year, but fresh in-season berries are so much better. It's the best combination of chocolate, fruit, and the classic oat bar.

MAKES 12, 1 bar per serving

1 cup all-purpose gluten-free or regular flour

½ cup old-fashioned oats

¼ cup unsweetened dark cocoa powder

½ cup oat or almond flour*

½ cup coconut or brown sugar

¼ tsp baking powder

¼ tsp baking soda

¼ tsp salt

½ cup melted coconut oil or unsalted butter of choice

1 tbsp vanilla extract

Filling

⅔ cup raspberry or strawberry jam

1 cup of whole raspberries or chopped strawberries

¼ cup chocolate semi-sweet chips

Preheat the oven to 350 degrees. Line an 8x8 or 9x9 square baking dish with parchment paper and spray with cooking spray.

In a medium bowl, mix together the flour, oats, cocoa powder, oat or almond flour, sugar, baking powder, baking soda, and salt. Pour in the coconut oil and vanilla extract and mix again. The mixture should be slightly crumbly but can hold together when pressed. Evenly press ¾ of the crust mixture into the baking dish with hands.

In another bowl, add the jam and microwave for 45 seconds. Fold in the berries and spread mixture in an even layer over the bar crust, leaving a 1-inch boarder around edges. Sprinkle with chocolate chips, then top with the remainder of the crust mixture. Press down the topping slightly to help it stick to the filling.

Bake bars for 35–40 minutes, until bubbly; bars will be soft. Cool in the pan for 1 hour, then transfer to refrigerator to cool for at least 2 hours.

Use a knife to separate the bars from the edges of the parchment. Remove the bars with the parchment paper to a cutting board to slice with a large knife into 12 bars. Serve warm or eat cold.

🥕 MODIFICATION TIP

*Oat flour can be bought or made simply in a high-powered blender. You can substitute almond flour for the oat flour, just keep in mind it will increase the calories and fat by about 2 grams.

Calories 243 | Carbs 31g | Fat 12g | Protein 3g | Fiber 3g | Sodium 15mg

Pizza Rolls

I have a few pizza recipes in this cookbook. Some are veggie-loaded and others just for fun. This is one of those fun Friday night treats. Fill with pizza toppings of choice. The best part is they are faster to make than you can call for pizza delivery!

SERVES 4, 2 eggs rolls per serving

1/2 cup jarred pizza sauce of choice

1 cup shredded dairy-free or regular mozzarella cheese

8 egg roll wrappers

Cooking spray or neutral oil for basting

Extra pizza sauce for dipping, optional

Pizza Filling Options
Spinach, sliced olives, chopped mushrooms, diced onions, or diced bell peppers

Add 1 tablespoon of the pizza sauce and 2 tablespoons of mozzarella cheese to the center of each egg roll wrapper. Add about 1/4 cup of additional pizza toppings of choice.

Fold in the side corners and then the end closest to you and roll forward like a burrito. Use enough water to seal the end of the roll. Do not pre-fill wrappers the day before or they will get soggy. You can fill it 1 hour before cooking if kept in refrigerator.

Spray the inside of the air fryer basket with cooking spray, add 4 rolls at a time and lightly spray or baste the top of rolls with oil. Cook at 400 degrees for 8–10 minutes or until golden, flipping halfway through. Repeat with the remainder of the rolls. Serve immediately with extra pizza sauce.

PREP TIP

Pizza rolls can be assembled and then frozen for up to one month. Cook from frozen at 370 degrees for 10–12 minutes or until golden.

COOKING TIP

If you don't have an air fryer, the pizza rolls can be baked in the oven at 400 degrees for 14–16 minutes, flipping halfway through cooking.

Calories 220 | Carbs 33g | Fat 8g | Protein 12g | Fiber 1g | Sodium 280mg

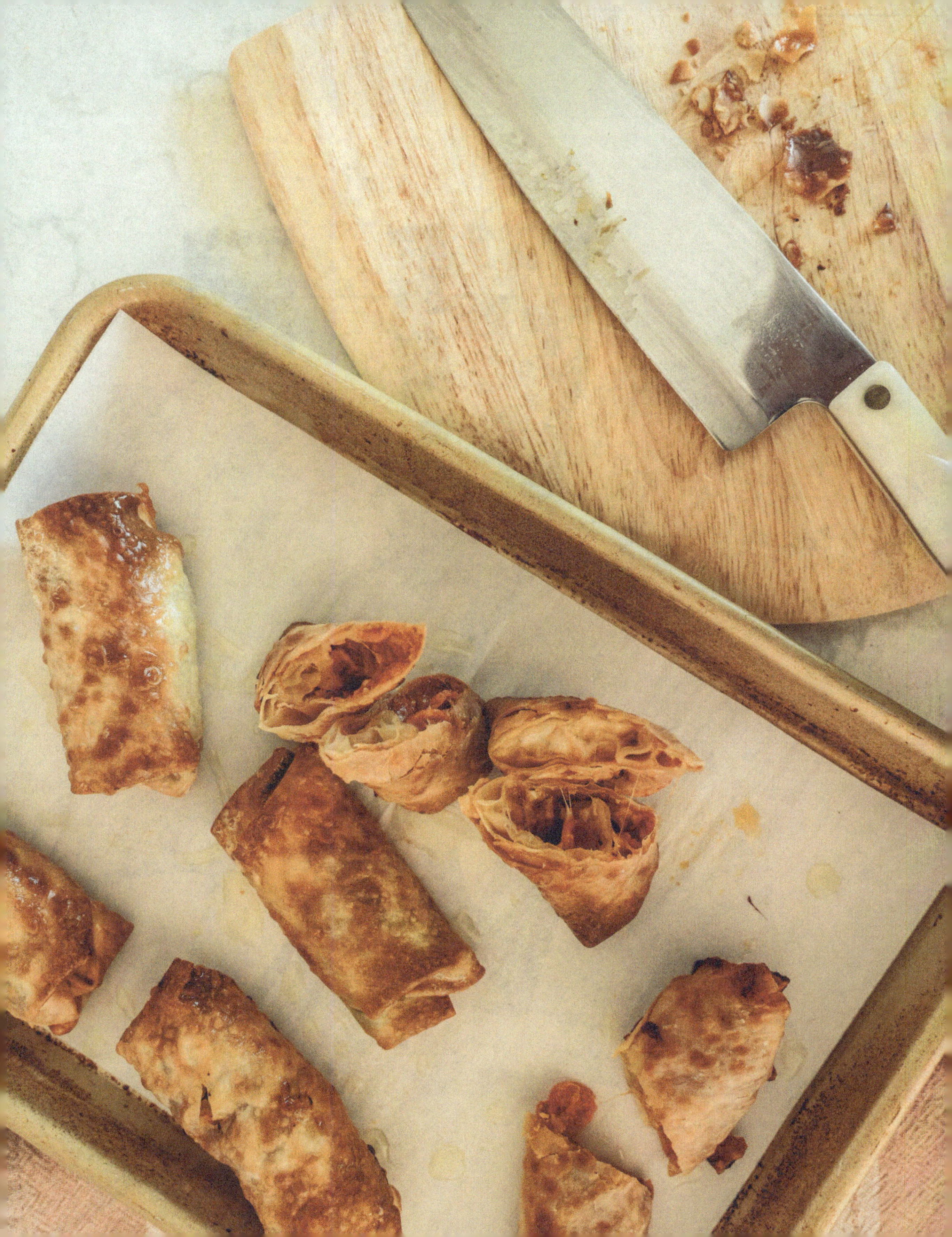

Protein Chocolate Chip Cookie Bars (page 46)

Chocolate Brownie Dip

This Chocolate Brownie Dip is like a sweet version of hummus. Don't worry, you can't taste the beans at all, but you will get the full health benefits from them. Serve this as a light, healthy treat, snack, or in cold lunches.

SERVES 6, 1/4 cup per serving

15 oz can garbanzo beans, rinsed and drained

1/3 cup unsweetened cocoa powder

2 tsp vanilla extract

3 tbsp unsweetened dairy-free or regular milk

1/4 coconut or brown sugar

1/4 cup maple syrup

Toppings
Chopped nuts and mini chocolate chips

Combine all the ingredients, except the toppings, in a food processor. Blend until very smooth, scraping down the sides as needed.

Transfer to a bowl and top with nuts and chocolate chips. Serve with fruit, pretzels, or graham crackers. Store in refrigerator.

MODIFICATION TIP

You can use any nuts for the topping that work well with chocolate such as pecans, macadamia nuts, walnuts or almonds. Make it simple and use raw nuts or fancy it up and use toasted nuts for more depth of flavor.

Calories 130 | Carbs 24g | Fat 2.5g | Protein 3g | Fiber 4g | Sodium 119mg

Strawberry Rhubarb Sauce

My husband's grandmother in Minnesota used to grow rhubarb and make this sauce every year. It's one of his favorite early summer treats. After she moved into a nursing home, I started making it to keep the tradition alive, adding a healthy spin to it, of course.

SERVES 10, 1/3 cup per serving

4 cups roughly chopped fresh strawberries

4 cups sliced rhubarb, 1/4-inch thick pieces, ends removed

3/4 cup honey or maple syrup

2 tbsp fresh lemon juice

1 tbsp vanilla extract

Pinch of salt

Add all the ingredients to a medium or large pot set to medium heat. Bring to a low simmer for 20 minutes or until fruit is broken down and tender and sauce is the thickness of chunky applesauce.

Allow to cool completely and refrigerate. Serve on top of ice cream or vanilla yogurt, in a parfait, or on its own.

MODIFICATION TIP

Substitute a cup of raspberries for part of the strawberries. It adds a bit more texture and sourness, but the combination is a nice alternative.

Calories 98 | Carbs 24g | Fat 0g | Protein 1g | Fiber 2g | Sodium 17mg

Jalapeño Popper Dip

This dip is great for a snack, game night, potluck or party. Serve it with some healthy vegetable dippers, pretzels, or tortilla chips.

SERVES 8, 1/4 cup per serving

8 oz container dairy-free or regular cream cheese

1/3 cup dairy-free or regular sour cream

2 tbsp mayonnaise of choice

1/4 cup water

1/4 cup mild or hot canned green chiles

1/2 cup shredded dairy-free or regular Monterey jack cheese

1 1/2 tsp garlic powder

1 tbsp fresh lime juice

2 tbsp nutritional yeast

Pinch of salt to taste

1/4 cup panko breadcrumbs

1/2 tbsp minced fresh jalapeños, optional

Topping
Chopped green onion

Preheat oven to 425 degrees.

Add all the ingredients to a medium mixing bowl, except the breadcrumbs, jalapeños, and green onion, and mix together well. Spread mixture evenly in an 8-inch round baking dish. Sprinkle the top with breadcrumbs and minced jalapeños.

Bake 12 minutes. Garnish with chopped green onion and serve hot or warm.

MODIFICATION TIP

This recipe can be made completely dairy-free. There are a lot of options now for dairy-free cream cheese and sour cream. They work as a great replacement for regular dairy products.

Calories 142 | Carbs 6g | Fat 11g | Protein 4g | Fiber 1g | Sodium 281mg

Snack Attack

Pucker-Up Lemon Hummus

I love my mom's hummus. She has made it for years to sell at farmer's markets and her customers love it too. I hope you enjoy making it your own by switching up the toppings and flavors!

SERVES 8, 1/3 cup per serving

2 ½ cups or 2 (15 oz) cans garbanzo beans, drained or cooked from dry

2 tsp minced garlic or 2 cloves, raw or roasted

2 tbsp extra virgin olive oil

1 ½ - 2 tbsp fresh lemon juice

½ tsp salt or to taste

1 tsp ground cumin

½ cup water or aquafaba (garbanzo bean liquid), or more to thin

Topping Options
Drizzle of olive oil

Sprinkle of smoked paprika

Chopped pine or Brazil nuts

Chopped fresh or dried herbs (parsley, cilantro, dill, or basil)

Lemon zest

Pinch of pink salt

Add the beans and garlic to a food processor. Pulse until coarsely chopped. Add the olive oil, lemon juice, salt, and cumin and pulse to combine.

While machine is on, pour in the water or aquafaba. Add more if needed for desired consistency. Check for seasoning, add more salt or lemon to taste.

Serve with topping suggestions of choice.

MODIFICATION TIP

Have fun changing up the flavors of your hummus! Add in some of these flavors to the first step: 2 tablespoons of tahini, 1 tablespoon of peanut butter, sesame oil instead of the olive oil, fresh herbs, lots of roasted garlic, fresh or roasted jalapeños, or canned roasted red peppers.

Calories 98 | Carbs 10g | Fat 4g | Protein 4g | Fiber 3g | Sodium 208mg

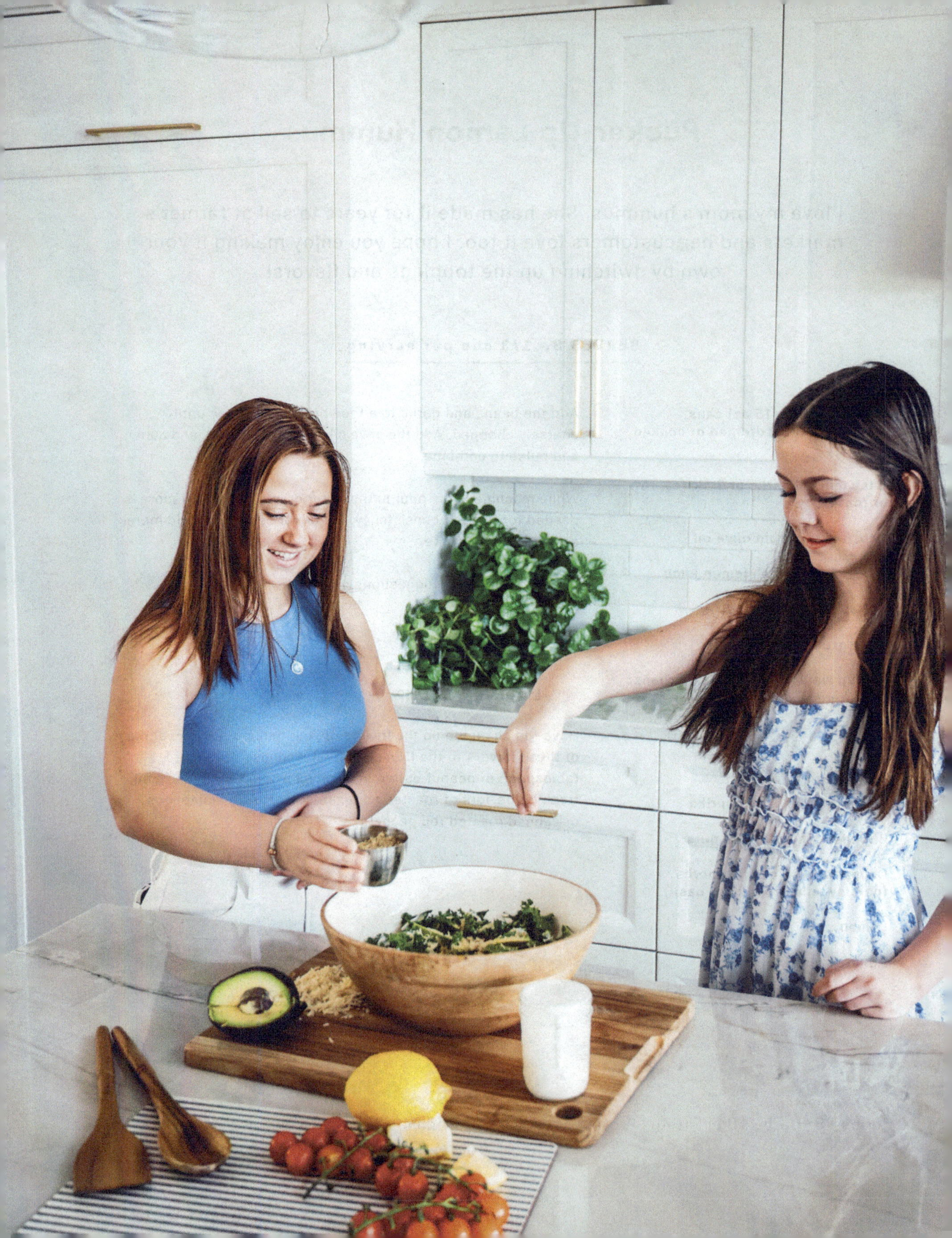

Veggie Loaded

California Kale Cesar Salad	**66**
Ginger Glazed Brussel Sprouts	**69**
Crispy Air Fryer Green Beans	**71**
Crispy Parmesan Broccoli	**72**
Strawberry Jicama Kale Salad	**74**
Spinach Palak Paneer	**75**
Mexican Enchilada Potatoes	**77**
Southern Collard Greens	**78**
Southern Cobb Salad with Creamy Ranch	**81**
Cauliflower Alfredo Sauce	**82**
Lemon Carrot Risotto	**83**
Crispy Smashed Potatoes	**84**

California Kale Caesar Salad

This is a great addition to any meal, as a side or a main dish. To accommodate each person of the family, serve everything separate and allow them to create their own salad.

SERVES 4, 2 tbsp of dressing per serving

Dressing
- 1/4 cup light or olive oil mayonnaise or low-fat yogurt
- 1/4 tsp pepper or more to taste
- 1 large clove garlic
- 1 tbsp Dijon mustard
- 1 1/2 tbsp small capers, drained
- 1 tbsp water
- Juice of half a lemon

Salad
- 4 cups packed chopped kale
- 1/2 cup snap peas, halved
- 1 cup cherry tomatoes, halved
- 2 tbsp ground walnuts
- 1 medium avocado, sliced

Topping
Shredded dairy-free or regular Parmesan

Add all dressing ingredients in a blender and blend until smooth, adding water if too thick. Set aside.

Add the kale to a bowl with the snap peas. Add half the dressing and toss to coat.

Add the cherry tomatoes and ground walnuts, toss again. Divide into four bowls and top each with avocado slices. Serve with Parmesan, if using, and extra dresssing.

Calories 169 | Carbs 14g | Fat 10g | Protein 5g | Fiber 6g | Sodium 300mg

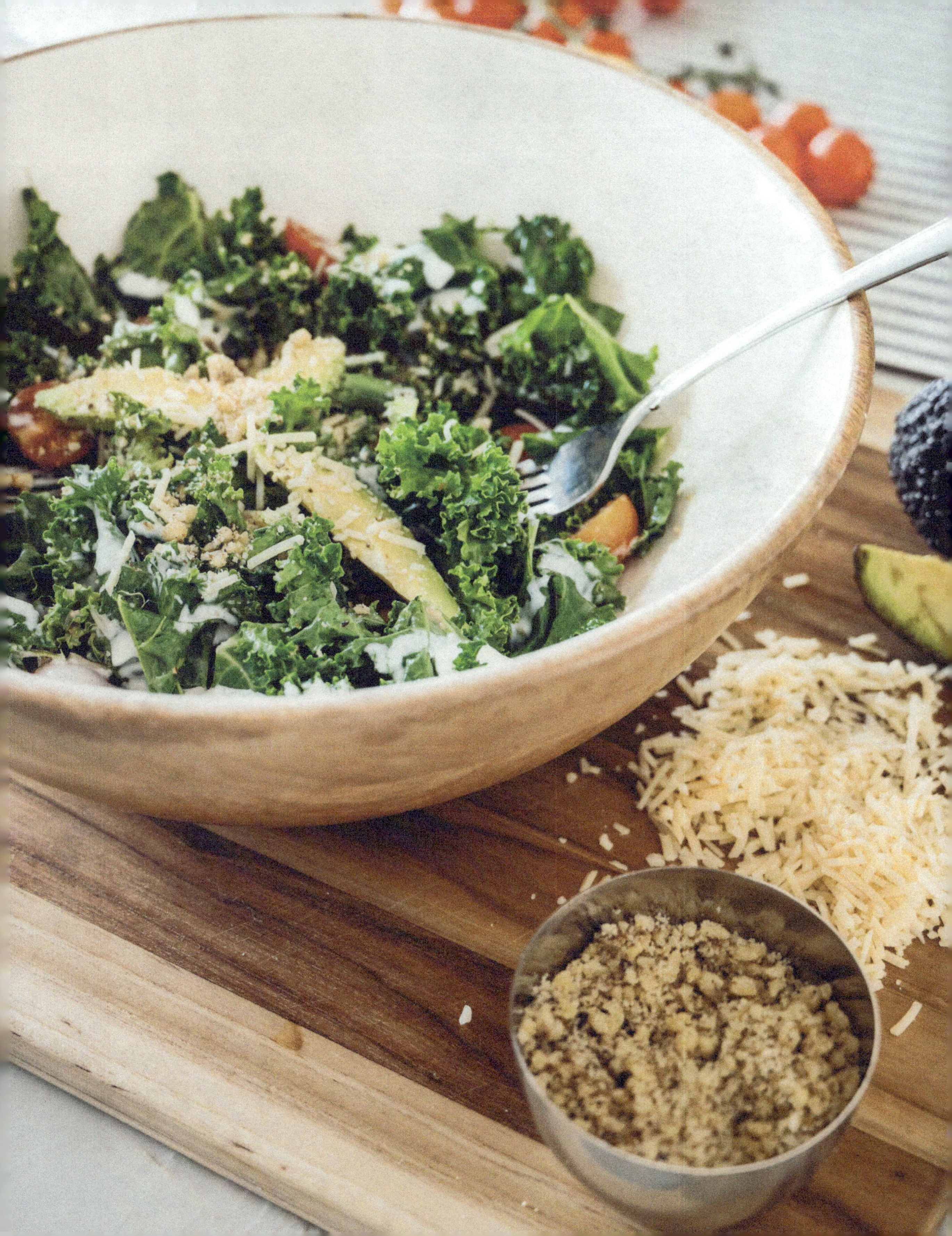

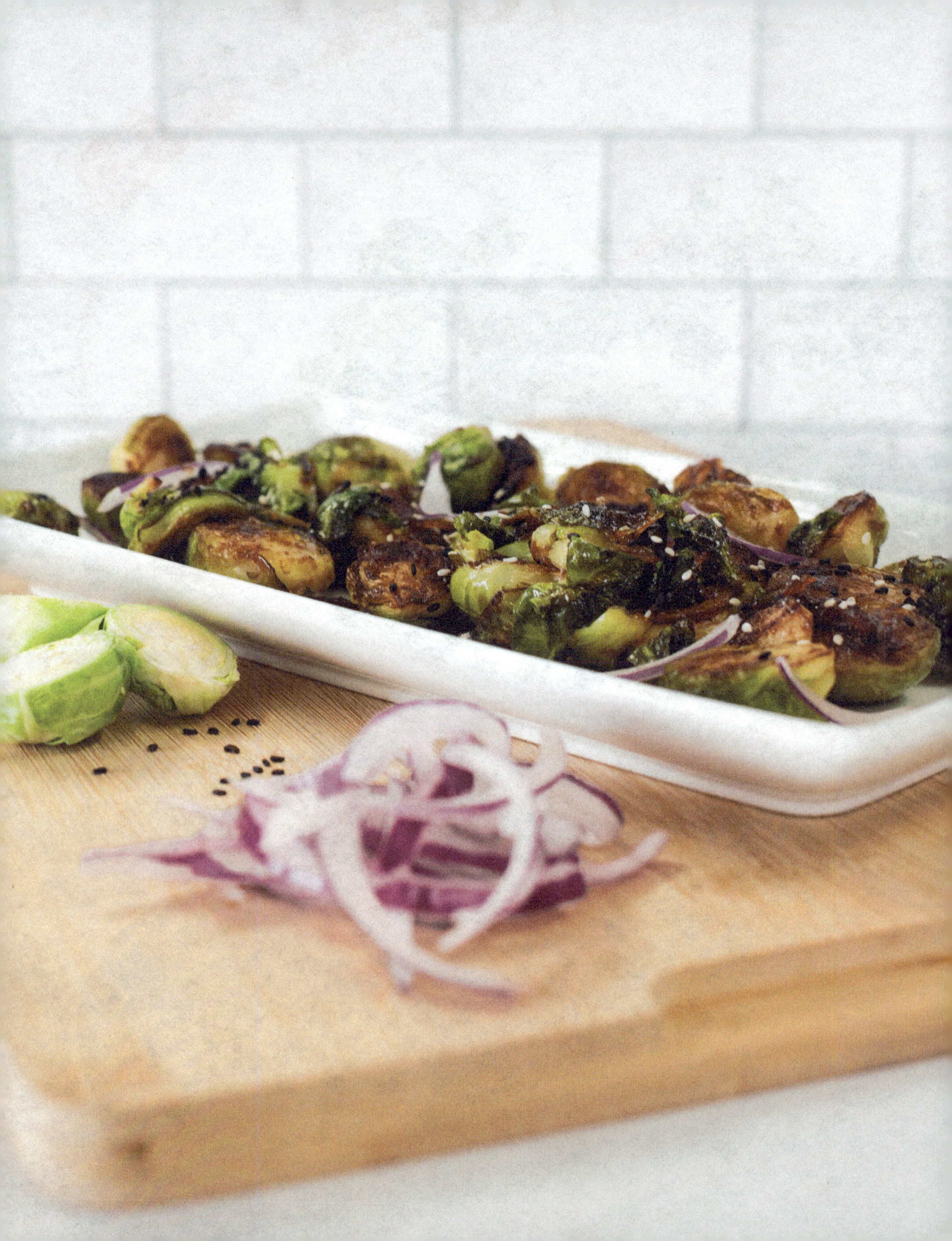

Ginger Glazed Brussel Sprouts

I didn't grow up liking Brussel sprouts, but if they had been prepared like this I would have loved them! One of my favorite go-to holiday recipes, this recipe will convert any Brussel sprout skeptic.

SERVES 6, 3/4 cup per serving

- 3 - 4 tbsp oil
- 20 oz Brussel sprouts, ends trimmed and cut in half (separate the leaves that fall off)
- 2 tbsp honey or maple syrup
- 1 tbsp ginger paste
- 3 tbsp low sodium soy sauce
- 3/4 cup sliced red onion
- Salt and pepper to taste
- Sesame seeds for garnish

Add oil to a large skillet with a lid and spread evenly on the bottom of the pan. Arrange Brussel sprouts cut side down in a flat layer and make sure to have a little oil on each Brussel sprout, do not overlap the sprouts. Set the skillet to medium heat, cover, and cook for 6 minutes.

Whisk together the honey or maple syrup, ginger, and soy sauce in a small bowl and set aside.

Add the sliced red onion and sprout leaves to the skillet; stir to combine. Toss the sprouts every 2 minutes for 8 total minutes, replacing the lid in between stirring.

Add the sauce and cook for another 2–3 minutes or until sprouts are glazed and fork-tender. Remove from heat, sprinkle with sesame seeds and serve.

COOKING TIP

The goal of cooking with the lid on is to steam the sprouts and begin to cook them through. They will have some color on the flat side. The leaves are removed before step one to keep them from burning.

Calories 149 | Carbs 14g | Fat 9g | Protein 4g | Fiber 4g | Sodium 346mg

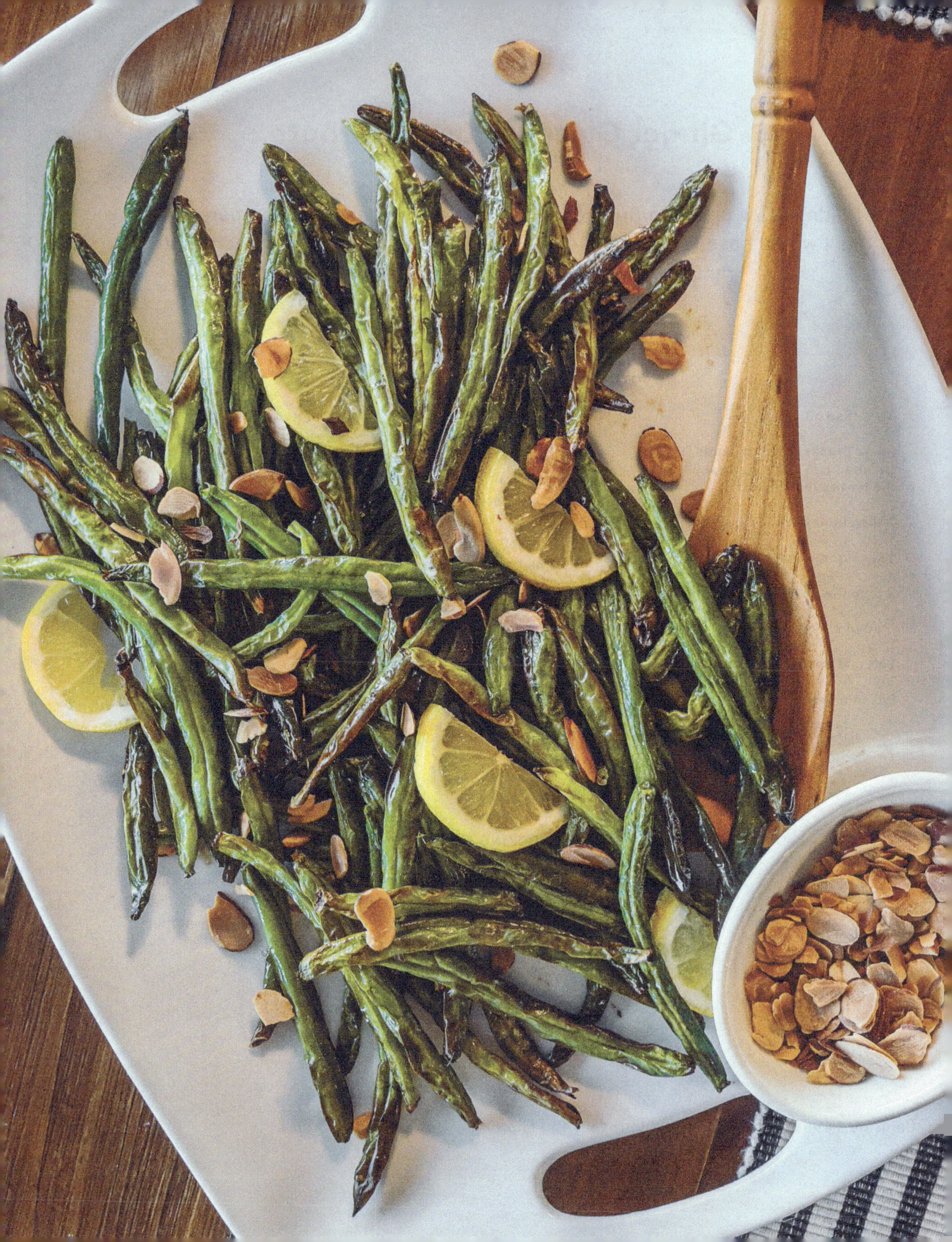

Crispy Air Fryer Green Beans

This simple green bean recipe will become your new weeknight side. Top with a squeeze of fresh lemon juice, chopped nuts, or fresh herbs, or just serve as is.

SERVES 4, 1/4 of recipe per serving

12 oz green beans, ends trimmed

1 tbsp neutral oil

1/2 tsp garlic powder

Salt and pepper to taste

Topping Options
Fresh lemon juice, chopped nuts, fresh herbs like parsley, or shredded dairy-free or regular Parmesan

Add the green beans, oil, garlic powder, salt, and pepper to a large plastic bag and shake to coat.

Transfer to the air fryer basket, spreading a layer over the bottom of the basket. You may need to cook in two batches, depending on the size of your basket.

Cook at 400 degrees for 8–10 minutes, shaking basket or tossing halfway through. Green beans should be tender and golden. Top with options and serve.

COOKING TIP

If using an oven to cook, preheat to 400 degrees and bake for 15–18 minutes or until crispy and golden.

Calories 59 | Carbs 6g | Fat 3g | Protein 2g | Fiber 2g | Sodium 151mg

Crispy Parmesan Broccoli

My daughter's favorite way to eat broccoli – crispy! Well, she calls it burnt; I call it extra crispy. Either way, this broccoli is delicious. Put this recipe on your weeknight menu rotation now!

SERVES 4, 1/4 of recipe per serving

2 large heads of broccoli, florets sliced*

2 tbsp neutral oil

Salt and pepper to taste

¼ cup shredded dairy-free or regular Parmesan cheese

Preheat oven to 425 degrees. Line a baking sheet with parchment.

In a plastic bag or bowl, toss the broccoli with the oil, salt, and pepper. Arrange on the baking sheet, flat side down, with some space between each piece. Roast for 12–14 minutes; broccoli should be tender and beginning to get crispy around the edges.

Remove from oven, toss, and then sprinkle the tops with Parmesan cheese. Roast again for 3–4 minutes or until cheese and broccoli are crispy and golden.

COOKING TIP

*Slicing the broccoli down the center of the floret gives it a flat side. The more surface area that is touching the baking sheet, the more golden that side gets. If some of your florets are bigger than others, slice them twice so they are a consistent size.

Calories 102 | Carbs 4g | Fat 8g | Protein 4g | Fiber 2g | Sodium 30mg

Veggie Loaded

CH 3

Strawberry Jicama Kale Salad

This salad packs in the fiber! Jicama, avocados, and strawberries are all great sources of fiber. Serve the toppings separately if introducing new foods to kids.

SERVES 4-6, 2 tbsp dressing per serving

Dressing

2 cups of whole strawberries, stems removed

1 tsp Dijon mustard

2 tbsp honey or agave

2 tbsp apple cider vinegar

1/8 tsp salt

2 tbsp neutral oil

2 tbsp water

1 tbsp poppy seeds

Salad

5 oz container of baby kale or kale mix

2 cups of quartered strawberries

1 cup blueberries

1 cup of julienned jicama

1 avocado, cubed or sliced

1/4 cup sliced almonds

To make dressing, place all dressing ingredients, except poppy seeds, in a blender or food processor and blend until smooth. Transfer dressing to a jar or measuring cup and stir in poppy seeds.

To make salad, arrange kale on a platter or in a bowl and top with strawberries, blueberries, jicama, and avocado. Top each portion with dressing and sliced almonds.

MODIFICATION TIP

Use any fresh berries to top the salad. You can substitute the jicama for cucumber, and the almonds for another chopped or sliced nut of choice.

Calories 218 | Carbs 19g | Fat 7g | Protein 3g | Fiber 7g | Sodium 55mg

Spinach Palak Paneer

Palak Paneer, also known as spinach curry, packs a punch of nutrition. The curry sauce base is blended spinach, which is high in iron and calcium. Substitute the tofu for paneer cheese, but it's truly worth giving the tofu a try. Its texture mimics paneer nicely!

SERVES 6, 3/4 cup per serving

Spinach Sauce

1 lb fresh spinach

1/4 tsp baking soda

1 1/4 cups canned coconut milk, shaken well

1 tsp ground fenugreek or 1 tbsp fenugreek leaves

2 tsp garam masala

2 tbsp Indian curry powder

Curry

2 tbsp neutral oil

1 tsp cumin seeds

1/2 small sweet onion, minced

4 cloves fresh garlic, minced

1 tbsp ginger paste

14 oz container extra firm tofu, cut into bite-sized cubes and patted dry

4 Roma tomatoes, diced and seeds removed (reserve 1/2 cup diced for garnish)

Salt to taste

Juice of half a lemon

1 tbsp ghee or unsalted butter of choice

Topping

Diced tomatoes

In a large skillet, wilt the spinach in 2 tablespoons of water. Add to a blender with the rest of the sauce ingredients and blend until smooth with some small pieces. Set aside.

Return the skillet to medium heat and add the oil. Add the cumin seeds, onion, garlic, ginger, and tofu. Sauté until slightly browned, about 5 minutes. Add the tomatoes and sauté another 2 minutes.

Add the spinach mixture and cook another 10 minutes on low heat, stirring frequently. Season with salt and squeeze of lemon at the end, about half of a lemon. Stir in the butter. Top each serving with reserved tomatoes.

PRODUCT TIP

Garam masala can be found in most grocery stores, but Indian curry powder is found best online. You can use a store-bought yellow curry powder, but the flavor of the Indian variety has more of an authentic taste.

COOKING TIP

The baking soda in the spinach sauce keeps the beautiful green color of the spinach while cooking.

MODIFICATION TIP

If someone in your family doesn't like onions, you can sauté them separately and blend them into the spinach sauce. Tomatoes can be left as a garnish instead of cooked in.

Calories 160 | Carbs 10g | Fat 10g | Protein 8g | Fiber 5g | Sodium 300mg

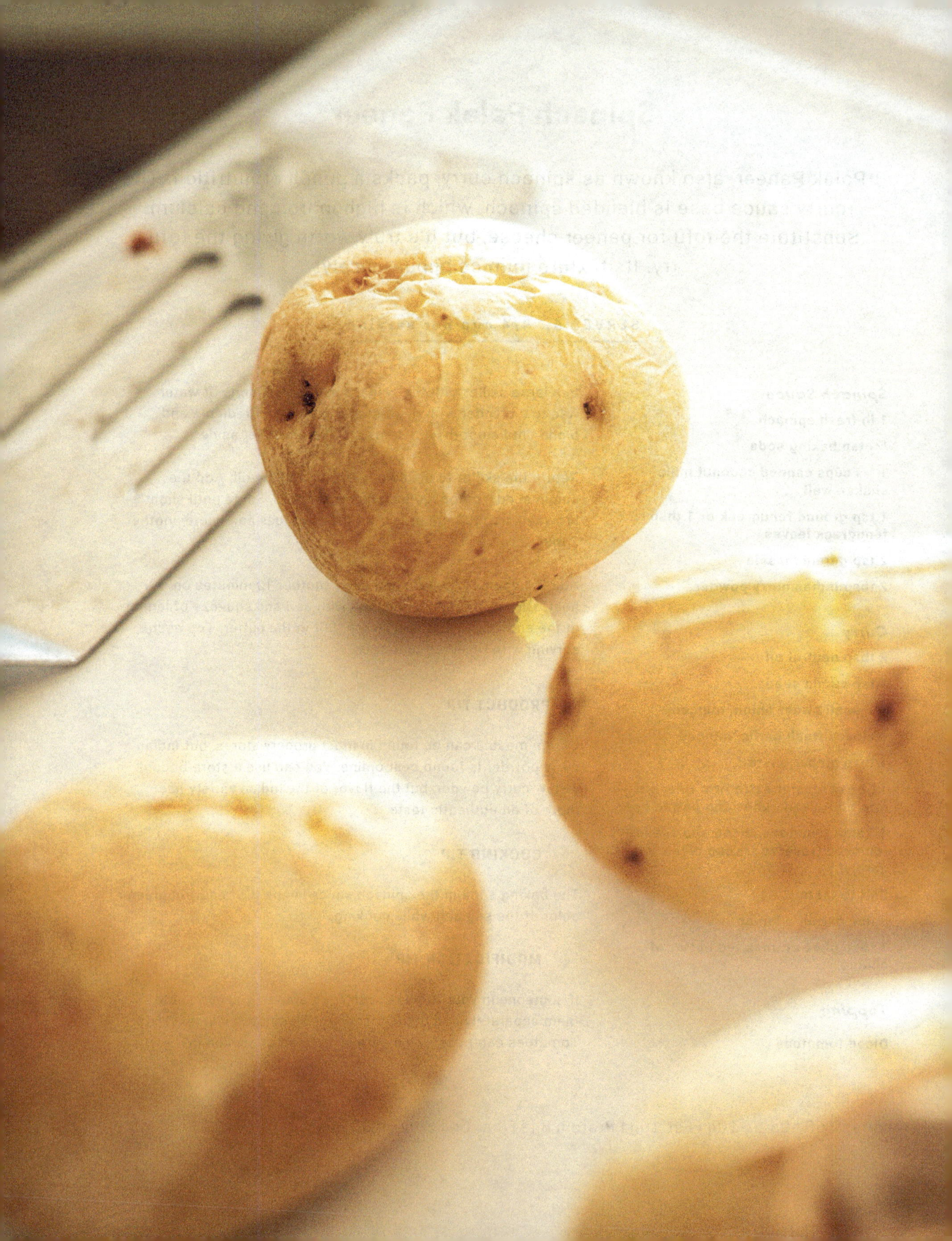

Mexican Enchilada Potatoes

These roasted potatoes are a simple and delicious side dish to spice up Taco Tuesday! Serve them as a filling for tacos, taco bowls, or as a side with a protein. Your family will gobble them up!

SERVES 4, 1/4 of recipe per serving

12 oz Yukon gold potatoes, large diced

1/2 cup sliced carrots or carrot chips

1/2 red or green bell pepper, cut into chunks

3 tbsp neutral oil

1 tsp chili powder

1 tsp smoked paprika

1 tsp dried oregano

1/2 tsp salt

1/2 cup enchilada sauce of choice

Preheat the oven to 450 degrees and line a baking sheet with parchment or silicone baking mat. Coat the potatoes, carrots, and peppers with the oil, chili powder, smoked paprika, oregano, and salt. Spread evenly on the baking sheet and roast for 12 minutes.

Remove pan from oven and toss potato mixture with enchilada sauce and roast again for 12 minutes or until tender and crispy. Toss halfway through cooking. Serve immediately or store for later use.

COOKING TIP

The potatoes should be starting to get fork-tender on the first bake. If not, cook them 2–4 more minutes, then continue on to step two. Add time on step two if needed, to get them nice and crispy.

Calories 179 | Carbs 20g | Fat 10g | Protein 3g | Fiber 3g | Sodium 480mg

Southern Collard Greens

I grew up in the South eating and loving collard greens. These might be new to your family, but make it a theme night! Serve the collard greens with **Southern Instant Pot Red Beans** (page 136) with rice and **Fluffy Cornbread Muffins** (page 51) for a fun way to create a southern-inspired meal and introduce new dishes!

SERVES 4, 1/4 of recipe per serving

2 cups vegetable broth

2 cloves fresh garlic, sliced

1/2 white or sweet onion, cut in half then thinly sliced

1 bunch collard greens, stems removed and cut into bite-size pieces

1 tbsp apple cider vinegar

1/2 tbsp jarred jalapeño liquid, optional

Salt and pepper to taste

Add the veggie broth, garlic, and onion to a large skillet set to medium heat. Once broth is hot, add the greens. Cover and cook for 15–20 minutes, stirring halfway through cooking. Greens should be tender with some bite to them.

Add the vinegar and jalapeño juice, if using. Season with salt and pepper, turn off heat and serve.

PRODUCT TIP

Collard greens can be found at most grocery stores in the organic produce section. They need to be washed well to remove dirt. Wash them the day before you need them for easy prep and cooking the next day.

Calories 46 | Carbs 4g | Fat 1g | Protein 2g | Fiber 1g | Sodium 200mg

Falafels with Tzatziki Sauce (page 144)

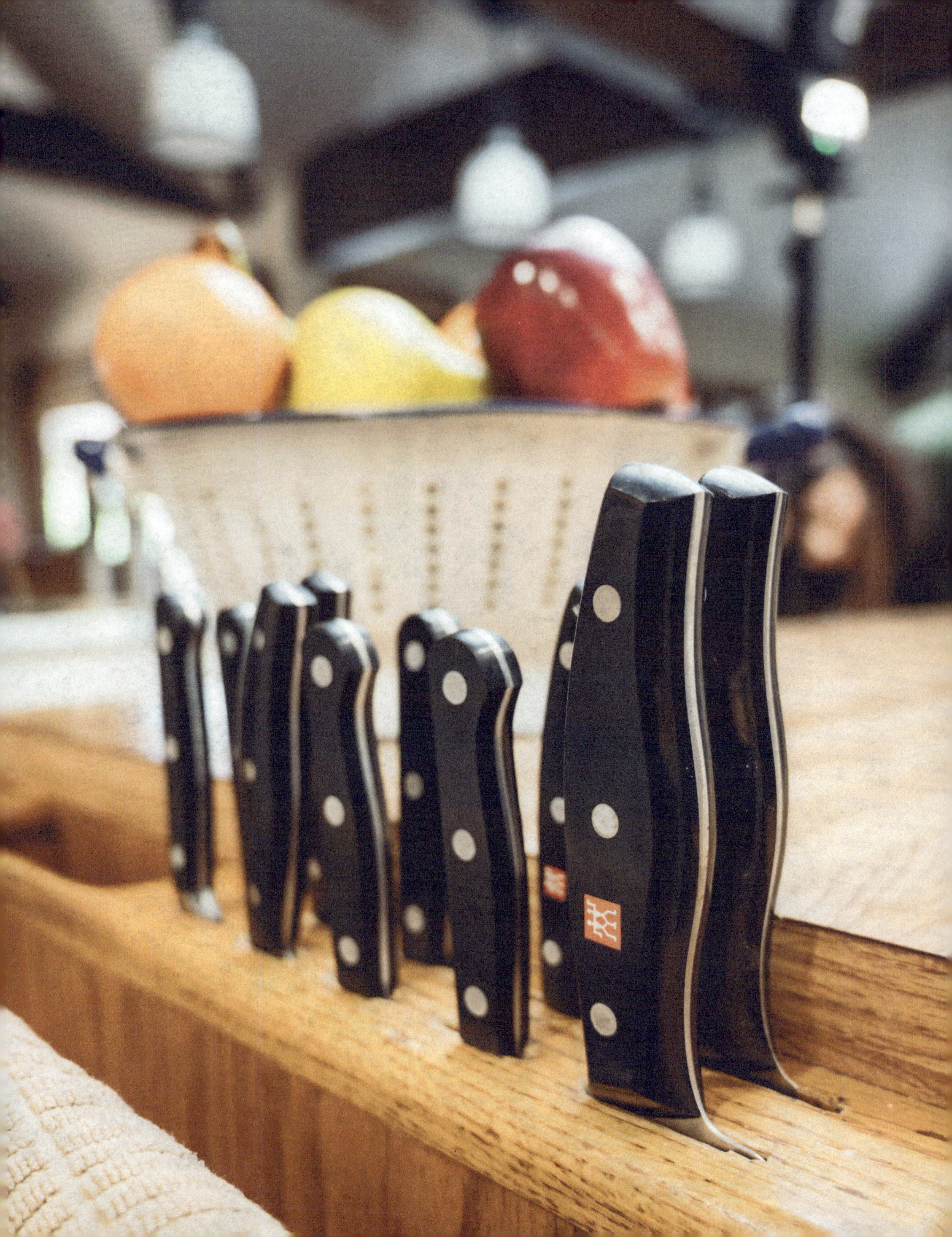

Southern Cobb Salad with Creamy Ranch

This is my take on a really yummy salad bar. I grew up eating at many southern buffets, and the salad bars back home were my favorite. There are so many bright colors and textures in this salad; it will remind your family of a rainbow!

SERVES 8, 2 tbsp of dressing per serving

Ranch dressing

½ cup mayo of choice

3 tbsp unsweetened plain dairy-free or regular milk*

2 tbsp rice vinegar

½ tsp celery salt

½ tsp dried parsley

½ tsp dried dill

½ tsp onion powder

½ tsp garlic powder

Salt and pepper to taste

Salad

9 oz chopped romaine lettuce

½ cup frozen peas, defrosted

½ cup frozen corn, defrosted

½ cup dairy-free or regular shredded cheddar cheese

1 cup pickled sweet beets

1 cup sliced cherry tomatoes

1 cup garbanzo beans

¼ cup sunflower seeds

¼ cup finely chopped red onion

Croutons, optional

To make the dressing, add all the dressing ingredients to a small bowl and whisk together. Set aside.

To assemble to salad, arrange the lettuce on a platter or on individual plates and arrange each of the ingredients on top in rows. Vary the colors so each row is different than the next. Serve the croutons and dressing on the side for each to top their own.

🛒 PRODUCT TIP

*I like oat or soy milk the best for a dairy-free option that does not have a strong flavor.

Calories 234 | Carbs 19g | Fat 15g | Protein 6g | Fiber 5g | Sodium 375mg

Cauliflower Alfredo Sauce

Use this simple Alfredo sauce for pizza or pasta; it's perfect for both! Bonus, you can't taste the cauliflower! I make the sauce thicker so it will stay on the pizza crust. Thin it out to desired consistency for pasta.

SERVES 6, 1/2 cup per serving

1 lb cauliflower florets, steamed or boiled until tender

1/3 cup whole raw cashews, soaked for 4 hours or boiled with cauliflower

2 tbsp lemon juice

1 tbsp pre-minced garlic

3/4 cup dairy-free or regular shredded mozzarella

1 tsp garlic powder

2 tsp Italian herb seasoning

1 cup vegetable broth*

1/4 cup dairy-free or regular heavy cream

Salt and pepper to taste

Add all ingredients to a high-powered blender and blend until very smooth. Add more broth to thin to desired consistency, if needed. Keep the sauce thicker for pizza. Refrigerate until ready to use.

PRODUCT TIP

There are great options for dairy-free cheese and heavy cream. I like Daiya brand for the cheese and Country Crock makes a plant cream that works great for this recipe.

*I like to use the Vegetarian Better Than Bouillon No Chicken Base for the vegetable broth. Make sure to pick a light-colored broth for most soups in this book. That will allow for the ingredients to shine and not get overpowered by the broth flavor.

Calories 132 | Carbs 7g | Fat 9g | Protein 6g | Fiber 3g | Sodium 135mg

Lemon Carrot Risotto

This might be my husband's and daughter's favorite rice dish. She used to hate carrots, which is why they are blended in some of the recipes, but now she will eat them if they are small enough. The carrots add a beautiful color to this recipe and their texture blends right in.

SERVES 6, 3/4 cup per serving

2 tbsp olive oil

2 tbsp butter of choice

1/3 heaping cup minced or small diced carrots

1 tbsp minced garlic

1/4 cup non-sweet white wine, optional*

1 cup arborio rice

4 1/2 cups vegetable broth, choose a lighter colored broth paste or carton broth, warmed

1/2 cup water, if needed

1/4 cup dairy-free or regular heavy cream

1/4 cup grated dairy-free or regular Parmesan

Zest and juice of one small lemon

Add the oil, butter, and carrots to a Dutch oven or deep skillet set to medium heat. Sauté for 3 minutes to tenderize the carrots. Add the garlic and white wine and cook for another 2 minutes or until alcohol has evaporated.

Add the rice and cook for 2 minutes. Add 1 cup of broth at a time and allow it to evaporate off before adding more. Stir frequently. The liquid should be at a low simmer. If it's boiling or simmering too much, turn down the heat. Repeat until the 4 1/2 cups of broth are used.

Check the rice for tenderness. If still firm, add another 1/2 cup water until rice is tender.

Add the heavy cream, Parmesan, and zest and juice of lemon. Stir well until creamy and liquid has thickened, about 5 minutes.

MODIFICATION TIP

*The wine is used to de-glaze the pan after sautéing. The alcohol cooks out but as an alternative, you can use more broth instead. The white wine does give it a nice depth of flavor for the foodies.

Calories 233 | Carbs 27g | Fat 11g | Protein 3g | Fiber 3g | Sodium 150mg

Crispy Smashed Potatoes

This recipe had to be in the book. I debated which section to put it in since there aren't any "added" vegetables with the potatoes. Nevertheless, potatoes are a root vegetable and are our family's favorite thing ever! These Crispy Smashed Potatoes always get devoured quickly!

SERVES 8, about 1/3 lb per person

3 lbs small baby reds or yellow potatoes

1 tbsp butter of choice

3 tbsp neutral oil

Salt and pepper to taste

Topping Options

Fresh chopped parsley and dairy-free or regular Parmesan

Bake whole potatoes on a metal baking pan at 400 degrees for 20 minutes or until fork-tender. Remove the potatoes from pan and transfer to a cutting board.

Melt the butter in the hot baking pan, then add the oil. Swirl around to combine and set aside.

Smash the warm potatoes with a flat-bottomed bowl or glass. Scrape potato off with a fork or knife. Don't worry if they break apart.

Divide butter and oil mixture into two baking pans. Transfer the potatoes back to the two baking pans, leaving some space in between. Baste the tops with the butter and oil.

Adjust the oven temperature to 425 degrees and roast potatoes for another 25–30 minutes until desired crispiness. Flip halfway through roasting.

Drain off oil, if needed, and sprinkle with salt, pepper, parsley, and shredded Parmesan.

COOKING TIP

Be sure to cook the potatoes until fork-tender on the first bake. After baking, potatoes should be warm for easy smashing. Apply even pressure when pressing the potatoes to keep them mostly together.

Calories 188 | Carbs 29g | Fat 7g | Protein 4g | Fiber 4g | Sodium 80mg

Veggie Loaded

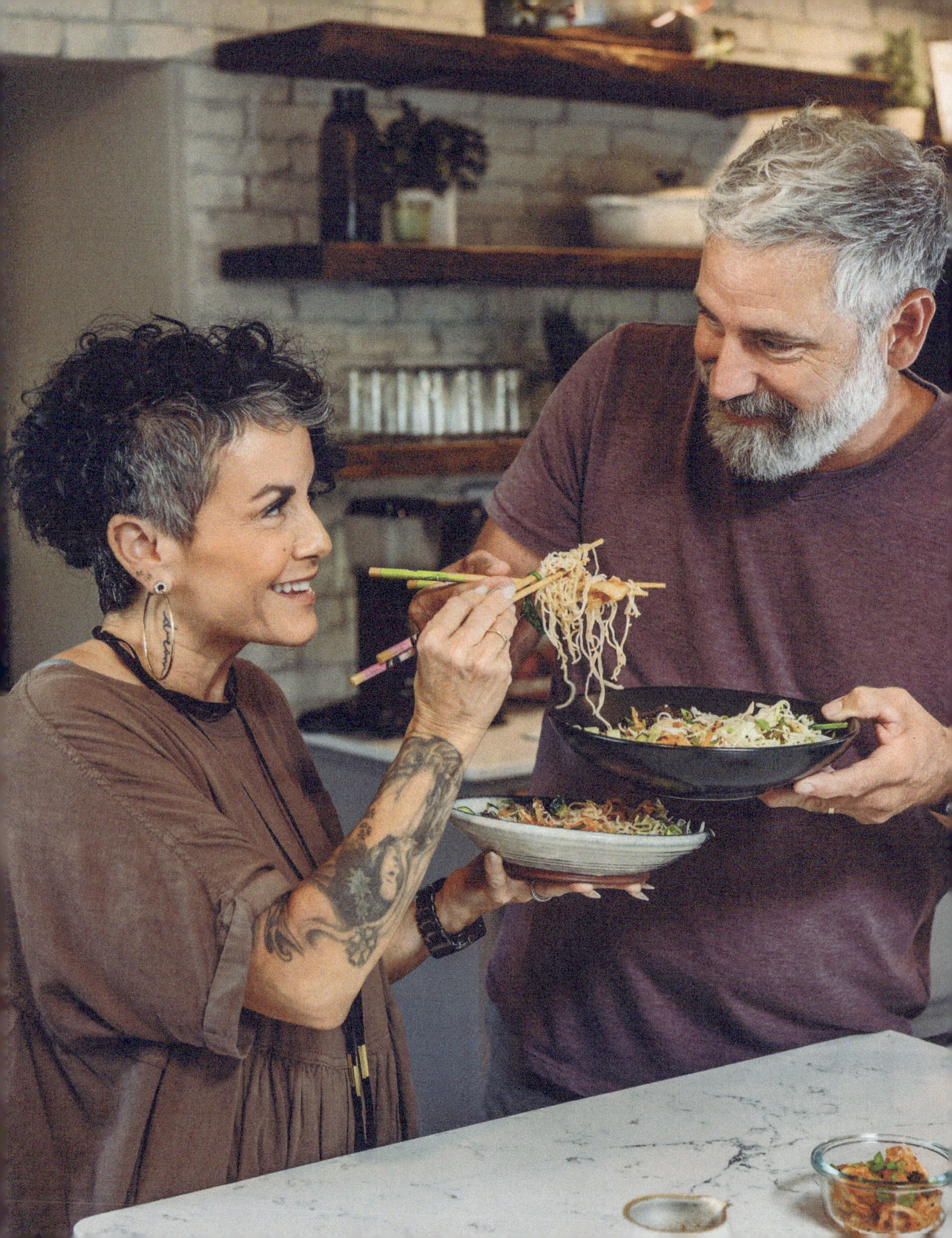

Adventurous Eaters

Pad Thai Noodle Bowl	**88**
Korean Ramen Bowl	**90**
Korean Baked Tofu Crumbles	**92**
Sweet and Sour Veggies	**93**
Pad Woon Sen (Thai Garlic Noodles)	**94**
Crispy Edamame Spring Rolls	**97**
Indian Potato and Pea Samosas	**98**
Apple Cheddar Grilled Cheese	**99**
Crispy Air Fryer Nuggets	**101**
Orange Sesame Tofu and Cabbage	**102**

Pad Thai Noodle Bowl

This is such a fun and easy take on the classic cooked Pad Thai. Served cold, this dish is perfect for lunches or warm summer days. Top with whatever vegetables and protein options your family likes!

SERVES 4, 2-3 tbsp of sauce per serving

Cooked rice noodles, about ¾ cup per serving

Pad Thai Sauce

2 tbsp tamarind paste

1 tbsp coconut sugar or brown sugar

3 tbsp coconut aminos

2 tbsp water

3 tbsp neutral oil

2 tbsp sweet chili sauce

1 tbsp maple syrup

1 - 2 tsp Sriracha or to taste

1 tbsp garlic paste or pre-minced garlic

Toppings

1 medium zucchini, thinly sliced

1 cup shredded green or purple cabbage

1 cup shredded carrots

1 cup chopped spinach

¼ cup chopped cilantro

¼ cup finely chopped peanuts

1 lime, cut into wedges

Cook your rice noodles according to package instructions. Make sure to rinse them well with cold water to remove the starch. If they start to stick together, rinse them again and toss with a little oil or lime juice.

For the sauce, whisk together all ingredients in a bowl and set aside.

Divide the cooled noodles among four bowls. Top in sections the zucchini, spinach, cabbage, and carrots. Drizzle on the sauce and garnish with the cilantro, peanuts, and lime wedge.

PREP TIP

Make the sauce and prepare the toppings ahead of time. Just before serving, cook the noodles, set out the prepared items, and allow each person to assemble their own bowls with their preferred toppings.

Calories 217 | Carbs 28g | Fat 15g | Protein 10g | Fiber 8g | Sodium 389mg

Pad Woon Sen (Thai Garlic Noodles) (page 94)

Korean Ramen Bowl

This bowl is a great way to expose your family to new flavors. Its mild Korean taste is perfect for young foodies. My eight-year-old absolutely loves it!

SERVES 4, 2 tbsp of sauce per serving

10 oz rice ramen noodles, cooked according to package instructions

Korean BBQ Sauce

1 - 2 tbsp gochujang (Korean chili paste)

2 tbsp sliced green onions

1 tbsp low sodium soy sauce or tamari

1 tbsp seasoned rice vinegar

1 tsp pre-minced garlic

2 tbsp coconut sugar or brown sugar

1 1/2 tbsp honey or agave

1 tbsp ginger paste

2 tbsp toasted sesame oil

1 tbsp water (if using as a marinade, leave this out)

Bowl

2 tbsp toasted sesame oil, divided

2 tbsp neutral cooking oil, divided

1 cup finely chopped mushrooms

3 cups raw spinach

1 tbsp jarred pre-minced garlic

Salt to taste

1 cup shredded cabbage

1 cup shredded carrots

1 cup small diced cucumber

In a small bowl, whisk together all the sauce ingredients and set aside.

Heat a skillet to medium heat. Add one tablespoon each of the sesame oil and neutral oil, then add the mushrooms. Sauté the mushrooms for 10–12 minutes, stirring every 2–3 minutes. Mushrooms should be cooked down and caramelized when done. Season with pinch of salt and set aside for bowl assembly.

Add the additional tablespoon of sesame oil and neutral oil to the skillet over medium heat. Add the spinach and a pinch of salt and sauté for 2 minutes or until spinach is wilted. Add garlic, toss to coat, and remove from heat. Set aside for bowl assembly.

Divide the cooked noodles among four bowls. Top in sections the mushrooms, spinach, cabbage, carrots, and cucumber. Drizzle with the sauce and garnish with kimchi, toasted sesame seeds, and green onions, if desired.

Toppings

Chopped kimchi, toasted sesame seeds, and chopped green onion

Calories 241 | Carbs 41g | Fat 7g | Protein 5g | Fiber 3g | Sodium 286mg

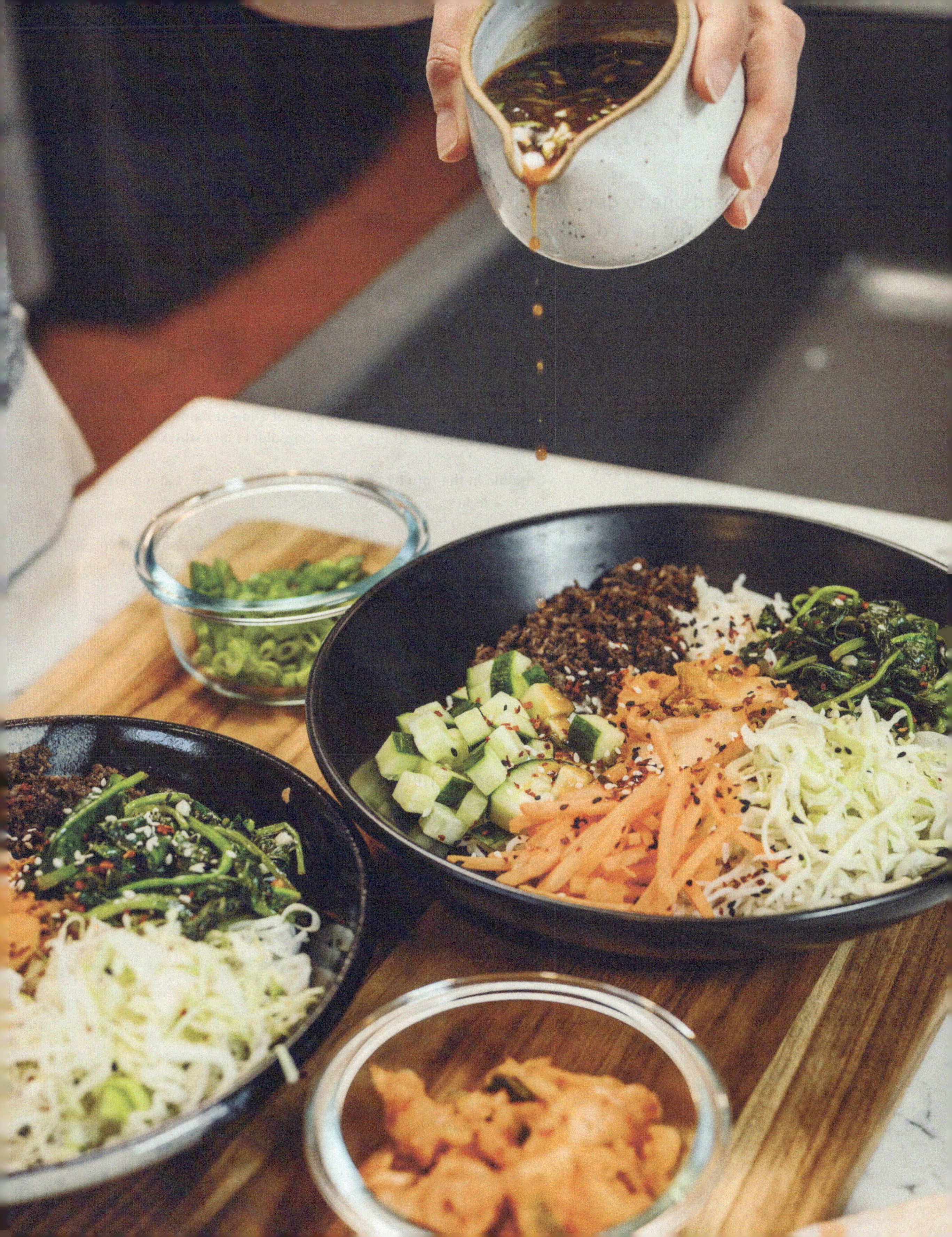

Korean Baked Tofu Crumbles

Tofu is a hard one to get past picky eaters. Cooked and seasoned the right way, tofu can be a delicious protein alternative even for the biggest skeptics. The Korean sauce can be used in a variety of dishes as a marinade, stir fry sauce, or basted on a grilled protein.

SERVES 4, 1/4 of recipe per serving

14 oz package extra firm tofu, drained and patted dry with towel

1 tbsp Korean style gochujang paste or sauce

½ tbsp corn or arrowroot starch

1 tbsp toasted sesame oil

1 tbsp maple syrup

1 tbsp coconut aminos

1 tbsp soy sauce or gluten-free tamari

1 tbsp seasoned rice vinegar

1 tbsp ginger paste

1 tbsp garlic paste

Drain and pat dry the tofu with a towel and set aside. In a medium bowl, add all the sauce ingredients and whisk together.

Crumble in the tofu by hand and toss in the sauce. Let marinate for 1–2 hours.

Spray a baking sheet with cooking spray or line with parchment. Baking time will depend on how dry the tofu is before marinating.

Bake for 30 minutes, tossing halfway through cooking. Add additional time as needed, tossing every 5 minutes. Tofu should be dry with some caramelization.

🛒 PRODUCT TIP

Extra firm tofu is best for stir frying, baking, or air frying. I always choose an organic brand to avoid the GMO soya beans tofu is made from.

Calories 168 | Carbs 10g | Fat 8g | Protein 11g | Fiber 2g | Sodium 417mg

Sweet and Sour Veggies

This healthier take on a restaurant classic is turned into a stir fry sauce for vegetables! Of course, feel free to use this on any compatible protein or vegetables of choice.

SERVES 6, 1/2 cup veggies with sauce per serving

Sauce

- 1/4 cup ketchup
- 3/4 cup water
- 1/4 cup honey or agave
- 3 tbsp seasoned rice vinegar
- 2 tbsp cornstarch or arrowroot starch
- 1 tbsp minced garlic
- 2 tbsp low sodium soy sauce or tamari
- 1/3 cup pineapple juice

Vegetables

- 1/2 tbsp toasted sesame oil
- 1 tbsp neutral oil
- 1/2 white onion, cut into chunks
- 1 orange or yellow bell pepper, cut into chunks
- 2 small heads of raw broccoli, florets only
- 6 oz green beans, cut into 2 - 3-inch pieces
- 1/2 tbsp minced garlic
- 1/2 tbsp ginger paste
- 1/2 tsp salt
- 1/2 tsp Chinese 5 spice, can omit if needed
- 1/2 cup vegetable broth
- 1/2 cup pineapple chunks

Place all sauce ingredients in a medium sized pot and whisk together. Heat pot to medium heat. Whisk often for 10 minutes or until sauce is thickened and can coat the back of a spoon. Remove from heat and set aside.

Heat a large skillet to medium-high and add both oils. When pan is hot, add onions and peppers and sauté for 3–4 minutes, tossing frequently.

Add in broccoli, green beans, garlic, ginger, salt, Chinese 5 spice, and broth, toss to coat all veggies and cover pan. Cook for 6–8 minutes or until veggies are fork-tender. Stir in 1/2 cup of pineapple chunks, serve over brown rice, and top with sweet and sour sauce.

MODIFICATION TIP

If adding a protein, sauté until browned first and remove from pan. Add back in after the veggies are done cooking to heat through and coat in the sauce.

Calories 141 | Carbs 26g | Fat 4g | Protein 3g | Fiber 3g | Sodium 422mg

Pad Woon Sen (Thai Garlic Noodles)

This yummy noodle dish is so simple to make and easy to modify. Any of the veggies can be left out or sautéed separately for those who want to add them to their own dish. For my picky eater, I stir fry the cooked noodles and sauce together and leave each veggie on the side for topping. If you have an adventurous family, I highly recommend making the recipe as is!

SERVES 8, about 1 cup per serving

6 oz package of glass or mung bean noodles

Sauce

¼ cup oyster sauce or mushroom oyster sauce

1 tbsp sweet soy sauce or coconut aminos

1 tbsp seasoned or garlic rice vinegar

1 tbsp honey or maple syrup

2 tbsp garlic paste or pre-minced garlic

Stir Fry

3 tbsp neutral oil, divided

½ cup carrot chips

2 cups sliced mushrooms

⅓ cup chopped onion

1 cup chopped green cabbage

1 small zucchini, cut into half rounds

1 large or 2 small Roma tomatoes, deseeded and sliced in wedges

½ cup green onion, cut into 1-inch pieces

Protein Options

Tofu, egg, or other

Bring a large pot of water to a boil. Cook the glass noodles for 8–10 minutes until al dente. Drain and rinse; set aside.

In a small bowl, whisk together the sauce ingredients and set aside.

In a large sauté pan, set to medium-high heat, add 2 tablespoons of oil followed by the carrots, mushrooms, and onions. Sauté for 6–8 minutes.

Add the cabbage, zucchini, and tomatoes and cook again for 3 minutes. Add the green onion, noodles, and sauce and cook for another 2 minutes, tossing well to combine.

PRODUCT TIPS

Glass or mung bean noodles are made from mung beans. They are easier to stir fry than a rice noodle because they hold their shape without breaking. Most grocery stores carry them in the Asian aisle, or you can find them on online.

Mushroom oyster sauce is a product you can find on Amazon or other online Asian food distributors. You can certainly use a traditional oyster sauce, but the flavor in the mushroom-based sauce is richer and less salty.

Calories 188 | Carbs 21g | Fat 10g | Protein 2g | Fiber 3g | Sodium 700mg

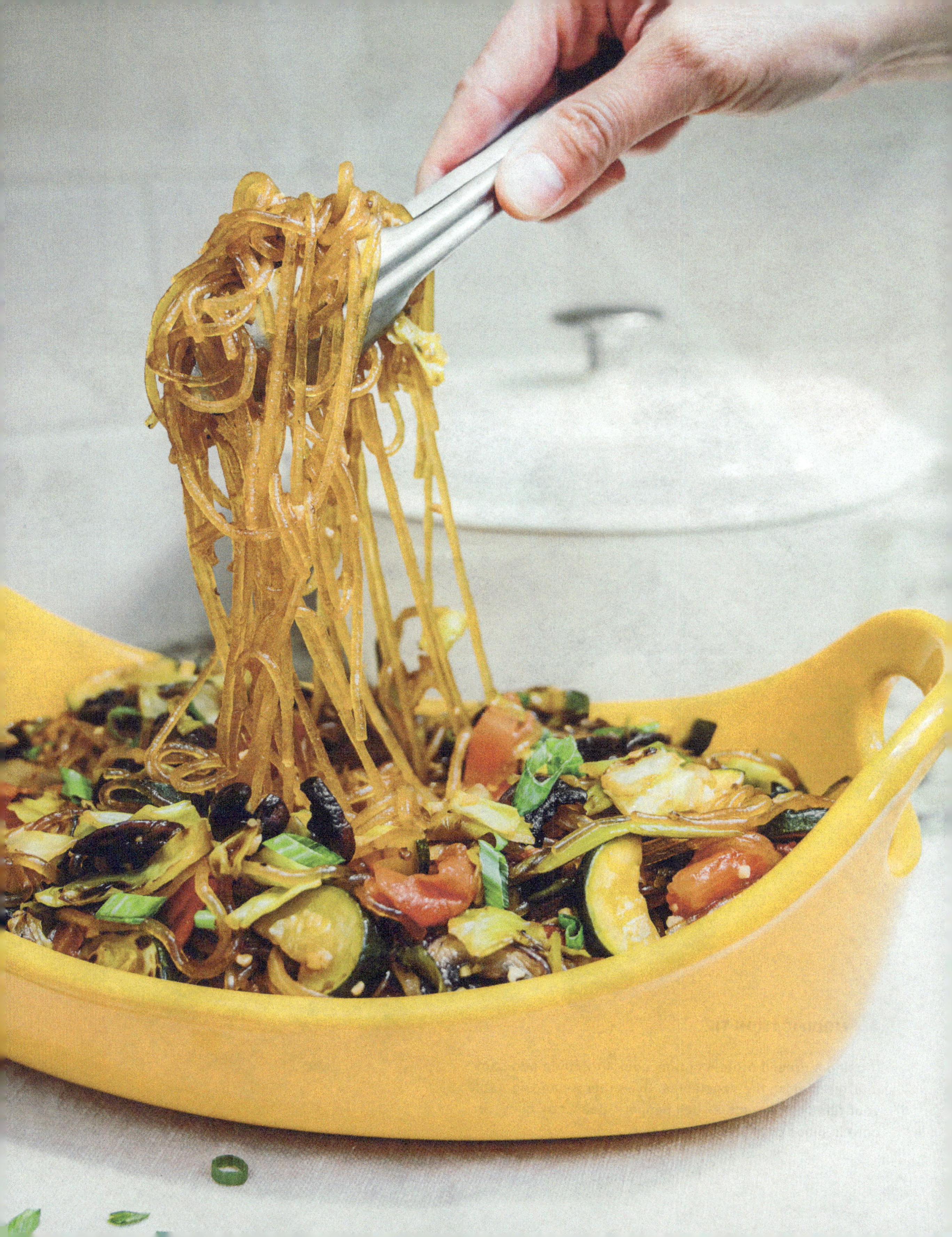

MODIFICATION TIP

If using a ground protein option, cook first, then add back in after cooking the vegetables. Use other Asian vegetables your family likes such as bell peppers, peas, bok choy, or corn in place of others in the recipe.

Crispy Edamame Spring Rolls

Crispy and filled with delicious veggies, these spring rolls are simple to make and totally customizable for your family! Feel free to experiment with other vegetables or a ground protein option for this restaurant treat at home!

SERVES 8, 2 rolls per serving

Filling

1 cup sliced mushrooms of choice (about 8 oz)

1 cup frozen shelled edamame, defrosted

1 cup matchstick, shredded, or finely chopped carrots

½ cup roughly chopped green onion

2 cups finely shredded green cabbage

2 tbsp neutral oil

1 tbsp ginger paste

1 tbsp minced garlic

1 tbsp low sodium soy sauce or tamari

1 tbsp seasoned rice vinegar

1 tbsp squeeze tube cilantro paste

Salt to taste

Spring Rolls

Phyllo dough frozen sheets, thawed according to package

½ cup oil for brushing

Thai sweet chili sauce of choice for dipping

Optional Topping

Cilantro for garnish

Add the mushrooms, edamame, carrots, and green onion to a food processor and chop until fine. Use the shredding blade on the food processor to shred the cabbage or shred by hand.

Heat a skillet to medium-high. Add the 2 tablespoons oil and all the veggies and cook for 5 minutes. Add the ginger paste, minced garlic, soy sauce, rice vinegar, and cilantro paste, and cook another minute. Remove from the heat and place mixture in a bowl to cool. Season with salt to taste.

When filling mixture has cooled completely and phyllo dough has defrosted, preheat the oven to 425 degrees and line a baking sheet with parchment.

Gently roll out the phyllo dough. Using a pastry brush, baste a light layer of oil on half the phyllo sheet and fold the other half on top. Place 3 level (or 2 heaping) tablespoons of the filling towards the top of one of the shorter edges in a 2-inch line. Fold the sides over the filling, then roll forward into an egg roll shape. Oil the edge, if needed, to seal. Place on baking sheet and repeat until all the filling is used.

Give each roll another light brush of oil on top. Bake for 15–20 minutes until rolls are crispy and browned. You may need to rotate pan halfway through, depending on the oven. Serve with sweet chili sauce and garnish with cilantro, if using.

🍲 COOKING TIP

If you have a smaller food processor, start with one vegetable at a time to chop into bits. If you put too much in, the blade won't chop the vegetables consistently and some will be bigger than others.

Without sauce
Calories 172 | Carbs 12g | Fat 12g | Protein 3g | Fiber 2g | Sodium 103mg

Indian Potato and Pea Samosas

Crunchy, light, and flavorful, these little samosas are a perfect dinner party appetizer or weeknight side dish. Filled with potatoes and peas, they are also a sneaky way to hide some veggies!

MAKES 18, 2 samosas per serving

1/2 lb baking potato, peeled and chopped into cubes

1/4 tsp ground cumin

1/4 tsp garlic powder

1/4 tsp curry powder

1/4 tsp ground coriander

1/4 tsp garam or tikka masala

1/2 tsp salt

1/4 cup finely chopped cilantro, plus extra for garnish

1/4 cup frozen green peas, defrosted

1 package square wonton wrappers

Cooking spray

Topping Options
Chopped cilantro and Indian chutney of choice

Preheat oven to 375 degrees. Line a baking sheet with parchment paper or aluminum foil and spray with cooking spray.

Cook potato in boiling water for 8 minutes or until tender, drain and cool.

Add the rest of the ingredients, except the peas and wrappers, to the cooked potatoes and combine, mashing the potatoes a little with a fork. You want some small chunks but mostly mashed. Stir in the peas.

Spoon 2 slightly heaping teaspoons of the potato mixture into center of each wonton wrapper. Moisten edges of the wrapper with water, bring 2 opposite corners together. Press edges together to seal, forming a triangle.

Place samosas on baking sheet and spray each side well with cooking spray. Repeat until all the mixture is used. Bake until crispy and golden for 12–14 minutes, turning halfway through. Top with cilantro and serve with your favorite Indian chutney.

MODIFICATION TIP

If your family is hesitant to mix vegetables together, serve the peas separately on the side and only fill with the potato and spices. Leave out the cilantro or just use it as a garnish.

Calories 138 | Carbs 26g | Fat 2g | Protein 4g | Fiber 4g | Sodium 300mg

Apple Cheddar Grilled Cheese

A foodie friend of mine introduced me to this flavor combination. Serve grilled cheese with the **Roasted Tomato Basil Feta Soup** (page 111). This is the perfect recipe to let everyone customize their own sandwich.

SERVES 2, 1/2 sandwich per serving

2 slices of sourdough bread

2 tbsp caramelized onions*

2 slices white cheddar or dairy-free option

2 tsp hot honey**

1/2 cup arugula or spinach

1/4 of an apple of choice, thinly sliced

Cooking spray

Heat a grill pan or panini maker to medium heat.

On one slice of the bread, spread the caramelized onions and top with one slice of cheese. On the other slice of bread, drizzle with hot honey, top with arugula and sliced apple. Put the two slices together.

Spray the grill pan or panini maker with cooking spray and grill on each side for 3–5 minutes or until bread is toasted and cheese is melted. Cut in half and serve warm.

EASY CARAMELIZED ONIONS RECIPE

*Peel and slice two large onions in half. Thinly slice each of the halves until you have a large pile of u-shaped onion strings. In a medium sauté pan, heat 3 tablespoons light olive oil or neutral oil over medium heat. Add the onions to the pan along with a generous pinch of kosher salt and black pepper. Stir constantly to combine the onions with the oil. When the onions are translucent and fragrant, turn the heat to a medium-low and continue cooking the onions until they are deeply brown and have reduced in size by over half. Stir every minute or so to ensure even cooking. Allow to cool to room temperature before using.

- Method by Andrea, The Salt and Stone Blog

PRODUCT TIP

**Hot honey is a nice spicy addition to a grilled cheese. Find it at most grocery stores or a local supplier.

Calories 210 | Carbs 30g | Fat 7g | Protein 8g | Fiber 2g | Sodium 225mg

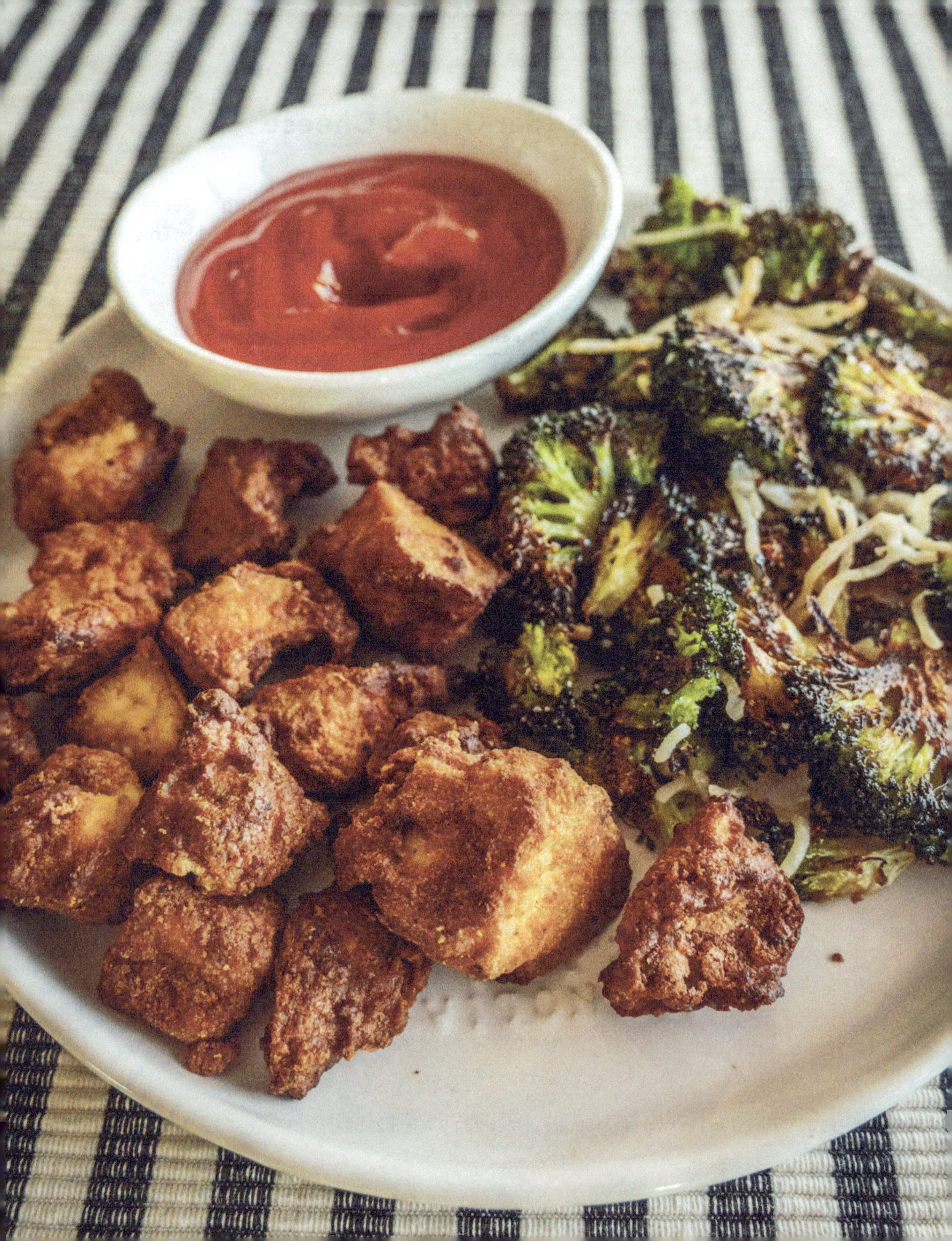

Crispy Air Fryer Nuggets

The coating on these nuggets gets extra crispy with the cornstarch and baking powder, making them a delicious alternative to traditional kid's nuggets. You can use the coating on other proteins but give these a try. I think you'll be pleasantly surprised that tofu can taste so good!

SERVES 4, 1/4 of the nuggets per serving

14 oz package extra firm tofu, drained and pressed of extra water

1/4 cup unsweetened plain dairy-free or regular milk

2 tbsp low-sodium soy sauce or gluten-free tamari

1 tbsp neutral oil

1/4 cup nutritional yeast

3 tbsp cornstarch or arrowroot starch

1/2 tsp baking powder

1 tsp garlic powder

1/2 tsp sweet paprika

1/2 tsp smoked paprika

1/2 tsp onion powder

1/4 tsp salt

1/8 - 1/4 tsp black pepper

1/8 - 1/4 tsp cayenne pepper, optional for spicy version

Cooking spray to coat air fryer

After tofu has been pressed (I recommend at least one hour in a tofu press), tear into 1-inch pieces of similar shape, comparable to the size of popcorn chicken. Set aside.

In a 9x9 baking dish, add the remaining ingredients and whisk together well. Toss the tofu pieces in the mixture gently until coated. Be careful not to break the tofu apart too much. Spread tofu on the bottom of the dish and set aside to marinade for 5–10 minutes.

Spray the air fryer basket liberally with cooking spray. Using tongs or hands, transfer the tofu to the basket, leaving some space between; it is alright if they touch a little. Spray the top of the nuggets with cooking spray.

Air fry the nuggets at 380 degrees for 15–18 minutes or until crispy, shaking the basket to toss halfway through cooking. Serve with dip of choice or store for later. Reheat in the air fryer.

PREP TIP

Tofu holds a lot of water. Pressing out as much of the water as possible is really important to get them crispy. A tofu press doesn't cost much, but if you don't have one, wrap the tofu in an absorbent towel and press it with something heavy on top. You can do this the morning of to save time. After it is pressed, place tofu pieces between two paper towels and press lightly to remove excess water.

COOKING TIP

To cook nuggets in the oven, bake at 400 degrees for 18–20 minutes or until crispy. Flip nuggets halfway through for even browning.

Calories 137 | Carbs 8g | Fat 4g | Protein 12g | Fiber 3g | Sodium 570mg

Orange Sesame Tofu and Cabbage

This is one of my favorite recipes from my earlier cooking classes. The lightly sweet orange sauce and crispy tofu makes a wonderful topping for fresh crunchy cabbage. Serve with brown rice for a super filling meal.

SERVES 4, about 1/2 cup of tofu per serving

14 oz package extra firm tofu, drained, cut into 1-inch cubes

3 tbsp cornstarch or arrowroot starch

Cooking spray

Sauce

1/2 tbsp cornstarch or arrowroot starch

2 tbsp agave or honey

1 tbsp rice vinegar

Pinch red pepper flakes, to taste

1/2 cup fresh or pulp-free orange juice

1 tsp orange zest

2 tbsp water

1 tbsp ginger paste

1 tbsp soy sauce or coconut aminos

1 tbsp sesame oil

2 cups shredded cabbage or coleslaw mix

Salt and pepper to taste

Toppings

Chopped green onion and sesame seeds

Preheat oven to 400 degrees. Place the drained cubed tofu on a paper towel-lined plate and pat dry. Allow to sit for 5 minutes.

Transfer tofu to a gallon storage bag with 3 tablespoons starch and toss to coat.

Arrange tofu on a baking sheet, leaving some space between pieces, and lightly coat with cooking spray. Bake for 20 minutes or until crispy, flipping once.

Add all the sauce ingredients to a medium sauce pot, bring to a simmer over medium heat, and whisk until sauce has thickened slightly.

When tofu is done, add immediately to the sauce and coat. Season tofu mixture with salt and pepper to taste.

Place cabbage on four plates or a serving platter. Pour the tofu on top of cabbage and garnish with chopped green onion and sesame seeds.

COOKING TIP

If using an air fryer, add tofu to basket, lightly coat with cooking spray, and cook for 400 degrees for 10–15 minutes, shaking basket halfway through cooking.

Calories 212 | Carbs 24g | Fat 8g | Protein 11g | Fiber 2g | Sodium 200mg

Adventurous Eaters

103

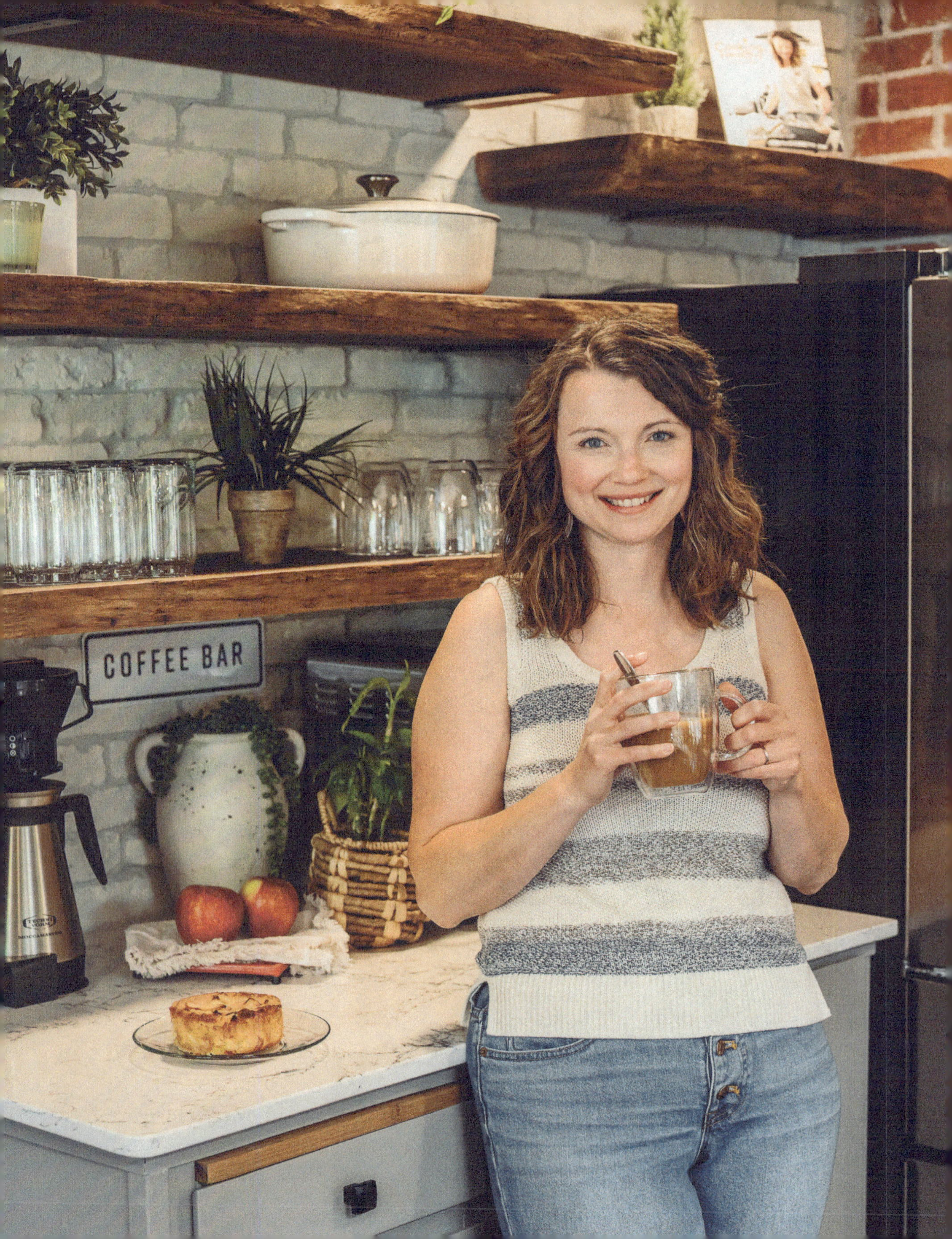
COFFEE BAR

Warm Soups

Instant Pot Split Pea Soup	**107**
Brazilian Black Bean Soup	**108**
Ginger Pumpkin Soup	**109**
Roasted Tomato Basil Feta Soup	**111**
Roasted Cauliflower, Leek, and Potato Soup	**112**
Tom Yum Soup	**114**
Tom Kha Soup (Coconut Soup)	**115**
Red Pozole	**116**

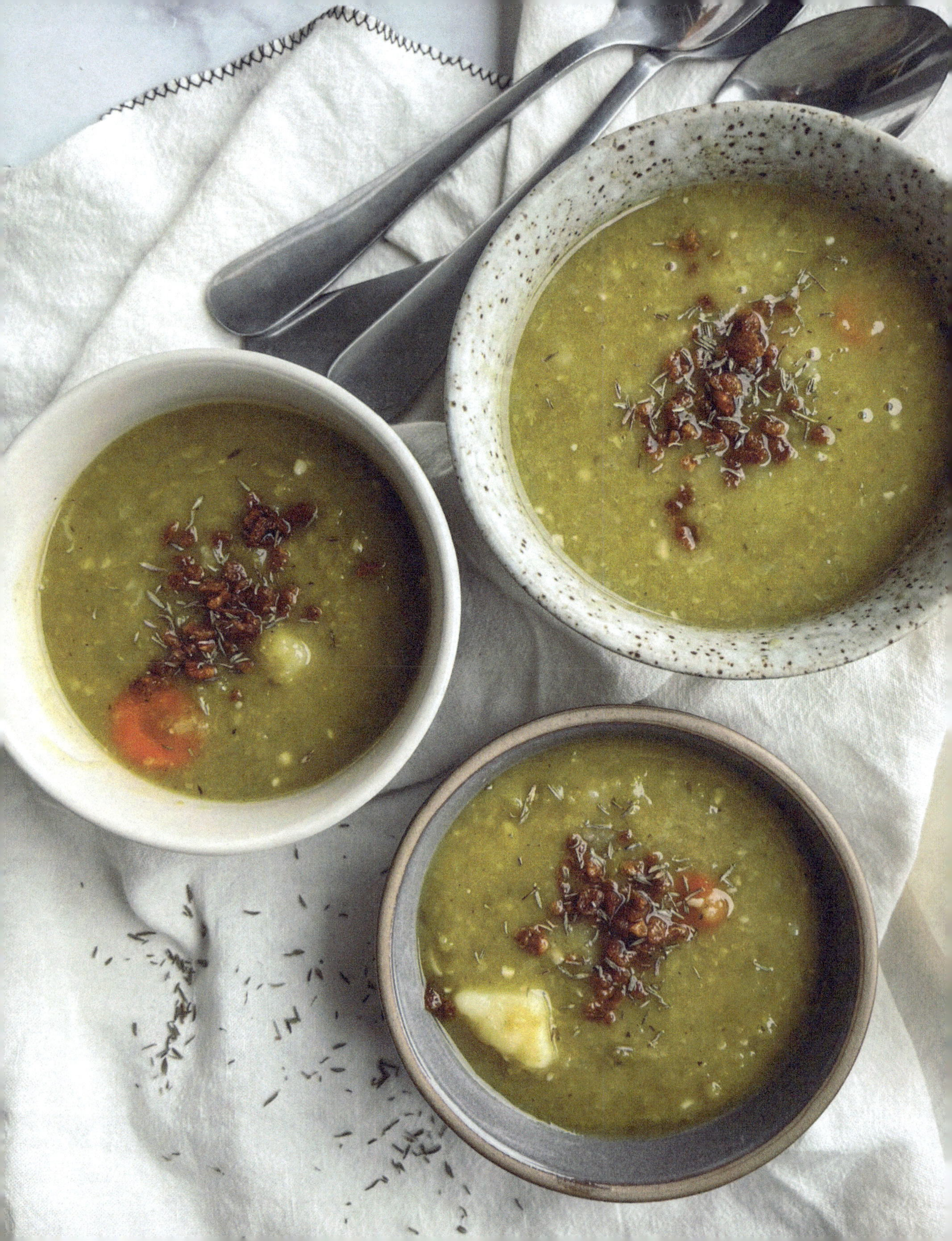

Instant Pot Split Pea Soup

Do not let the green color deter you from making this soup. I was so surprised at how much my daughter loved it.

SERVES 8, 1 cup per serving

2 tbsp neutral oil

1/2 medium yellow or sweet onion, minced

1 large carrot, peeled and sliced thin

1 1/2 tbsp minced garlic

1/2 tsp ground thyme

1/2 tsp poultry seasoning

1/2 tsp celery salt

1 lb dried green split peas, rinsed and sorted

1 large russet potato, peeled and diced small

1/4 tsp black pepper

1 1/2 tbsp hickory liquid smoke

5 cups light-colored vegetable broth

1 1/2 cup water

Toppings
Textured vegetable protein (TVP) Bacon Bits*

Turn on the instant pot to medium sauté and add the oil, onions, and carrot. Cook for 5 minutes. Add the garlic, thyme, poultry seasoning, and celery salt and sauté again for 2 minutes. Add the rest of the soup ingredients and stir well to combine.

Turn the instant pot off, then set to manual high pressure for 18 minutes. Manually release the steam and check for seasoning. If using the TVP Bacon, don't over salt the soup as bacon bits are already salty.

HOW TO MAKE TVP BACON BITS

*In a bowl, mix together 1/2 tbsp Worcestershire sauce, 1 tbsp coconut sugar, 1 tbsp maple syrup, 1 tbsp oil, 2 tbsp soy sauce, 1 1/2 tbsp liquid smoke, 1 tsp granulated garlic, and 1/4 tsp salt. Toss 1 cup textured vegetable protein with the sauce and let sit for 5 minutes. Preheat oven to 300 degrees, spread mixture on a parchment-lined baking sheet, and bake for 12–15 minutes, stirring halfway through. Transfer to a bowl to cool.

MODIFICATION TIP

When I first introduced this soup to my daughter, I left out the carrots. The onions and garlic really blend in well and, if cut small enough, are undetectable to even the pickiest of kids. I encourage making the TVP bacon bits and leaving them on the side for them to try separately or sprinkle on themselves. You'll be amazed at how delicious it is!

Calories 301 | Carbs 55g | Fat 5g | Protein 16g | Fiber 17g | Sodium 600mg

Brazilian Black Bean Soup

This is an older recipe that I use over and over. My health coaching clients love it. It's low fat, creamy, full of protein, fiber, and the vegetables just blend right in.

SERVES 6, 1 cup per serving

3 (15 oz) cans black beans, drained

1 small sweet onion, diced

1 cup matchstick carrots

3 cups vegetable broth

2 tbsp tomato paste

2 tbsp minced garlic

2 tbsp molasses

1 tbsp smoked paprika

½ tbsp ground cumin

½ tbsp dried oregano

¼ tsp chipotle powder, optional

2 cups kale, finely chopped

Juice of one lime

Topping Options

2 Roma tomatoes, diced

Sour cream

Heat a pot to medium heat. Add all ingredients through chipotle powder to the pot. Stir to combine. Cook for 15 minutes, stirring occasionally.

Take soup off the heat. Using an immersion blender, purée some of the soup. Alternatively, use a standing blender to purée half of the soup, then return to the pot.

Return the soup to medium heat and add the kale. Cook for another 1–2 minutes, just enough to cook down the kale a bit, and then add the lime juice.

Portion soup into bowls and top with diced tomato and sour cream.

PREP TIP

The best way I have found to get the kale small is in a food processor. I recommend investing in an inexpensive one. It will save you so much time in the kitchen.

Calories 238 | Carbs 44g | Fat 0g | Protein 12g | Fiber 9g | Sodium 600mg

Ginger Pumpkin Soup

Probably the most loved soup in our home, this slightly sweet and savory soup is great for lunch or dinner. Serve with a family-approved side dish for a warm, healthy meal that is sure to please everyone!

SERVES 4, 1 cup per serving

2 tbsp neutral oil

1 Honeycrisp, Gala or red cooking apple, skin on and cut in chunks

½ sweet onion, cut in chunks

3-inch piece of peeled ginger, chopped small

2 cloves fresh garlic, peeled and left whole

1 - 1 ½ cups light-flavored vegetable broth

2 tsp honey or maple syrup

15 oz can pumpkin puree

1 cup canned full-fat coconut milk, reserve the rest for garnish

Salt and pepper to taste

Toppings
Cayenne pepper, diced apple, pumpkin seeds, coconut milk drizzle

Set a soup pot to medium heat and add the oil. Add the apple, onion, ginger, garlic, and sauté about 18–20 minutes or until ingredients have softened and caramelized to a golden color.

Add the veggie broth, honey, and pumpkin puree and simmer for 5 minutes. Add the coconut milk and remove from heat. Transfer the soup to a blender pitcher and blend it for a smoother soup. Make sure to vent the lid to avoid it popping off from the steam.

Transfer back to the pot and heat again, if needed. Season with salt and pepper and divide the soup into bowls. Garnish with suggested toppings and serve.

PRODUCT TIP

I like to use the Vegetarian Better Than Bouillon No Chicken Base for the vegetable broth. Make sure to pick a light-colored broth for most soups in this book. That will allow for the ingredients to shine and not get overpowered by the broth flavor.

COOKING TIP

The most important step in this recipe is the first one. Please don't rush the caramelization process; it is needed to increase the richness of the soup. Since there are no spices added, this is where the flavor comes from.

Without garnish
Calories 284 | Carbs 27g | Fat 18g | Protein 3g | Fiber 2g | Sodium 400mg

Warm Soups

Roasted Tomato Basil Feta Soup

This recipe was inspired by a TikTok video I saw for Feta Tomato Pasta. I made it into a soup and changed the feta to just a garnish. This will become your new favorite tomato soup recipe year-round!

SERVES 6, 3/4 cup per serving

8 Roma or on-the-vine tomatoes, cut in half or quartered if larger than a Roma

1/2 large sweet onion, cut in chunks

4 cloves fresh garlic, peeled and left whole

2 tbsp olive oil

Salt and pepper to taste

1/2 tbsp dried thyme leaves

1 cup vegetable broth

1 cup canned light coconut milk, shaken or mixed well

2 tbsp tomato paste

1/4 cup packed fresh basil leaves

Toppings
Feta cheese, chopped or julienned basil, red pepper flakes

Preheat the oven to 400 degrees. Line a large baking sheet with foil. Add the tomatoes, onion, and garlic to the pan, then drizzle with olive oil and sprinkle with salt, pepper, and thyme. Roast for 40 minutes, stirring halfway through.

Add the roasted veggies, broth, coconut milk, and tomato paste to a blender and purée. Add the fresh basil, salt, and pepper and blend again until basil is in small pieces. Heat to serve. Top with garnish options.

SERVING TIP

The garnishes with the soup are amazing, but some kids may prefer the soup without the toppings and that is totally fine too!

Without garnish
Calories 148 | Carbs 8g | Fat 11g | Protein 3g | Fiber 2g | Sodium 155mg

Roasted Cauliflower, Leek, and Potato Soup

Mixing cauliflower with potatoes is a great way to introduce a new vegetable. On its own, cauliflower can be a strong taste. Roasting it until golden and blending it with potatoes will make it much yummier and hopefully it will be a new favorite vegetable!

SERVES 6, 1 cup per serving

32 oz fresh cauliflower florets, cut into bite-sized pieces

5 tbsp olive oil, divided

3 tbsp butter of choice, divided

2 leeks, cut in half lengthwise, and chopped*

4 cloves fresh garlic, minced

1 tsp finely chopped fresh rosemary

2 medium (about 10 oz) Yukon gold potatoes, peeled and diced small

4 ½ - 5 cups vegetable broth**

Salt and pepper to taste

Toppings
Roasted cauliflower, shredded dairy-free or regular Parmesan, dried chives

PRODUCT TIP

**I used Vegetarian Better Than Bouillon No Chicken Base for the broth. You can use any light-colored vegetable broth you like.

Preheat the oven to 450 degrees. Line a baking sheet with parchment paper. Toss cauliflower with 3 tablespoons of olive oil, salt and pepper. Transfer to a baking sheet, without overlapping the florets. Roast for 25 minutes or until golden, tossing halfway through. Reserve 1 cup of the roasted cauliflower for garnish. Set the rest aside.

In a large soup pot, add the remaining oil, 2 tablespoons butter, leeks, garlic, and rosemary and sauté for 10 minutes on medium heat, stirring occasionally.

Add the potatoes and vegetable broth to the pot and turn heat to high. Bring to a boil, then reduce to a simmer until potatoes are fork-tender, about 12 minutes.

Using an immersion blender, blend soup until smooth. Season with salt and pepper. Stir in 1 tablespoon butter. Top each serving with garnish suggestions.

COOKING TIPS

*To wash leeks, cut the darker green ends off and trim the stem end. Cut in half lengthwise and wash in between leaves to remove any dirt. Do this thoroughly as leeks hold a lot of dirt inside the leaves.

An immersion blender works best to blend the soup and keep the potatoes from getting too starchy. Optional to use a food processor, but I do not recommend using a blender.

Without garnish
Calories 182 | Carbs 16g | Fat 12g | Protein 3g | Fiber 3g | Sodium 432mg

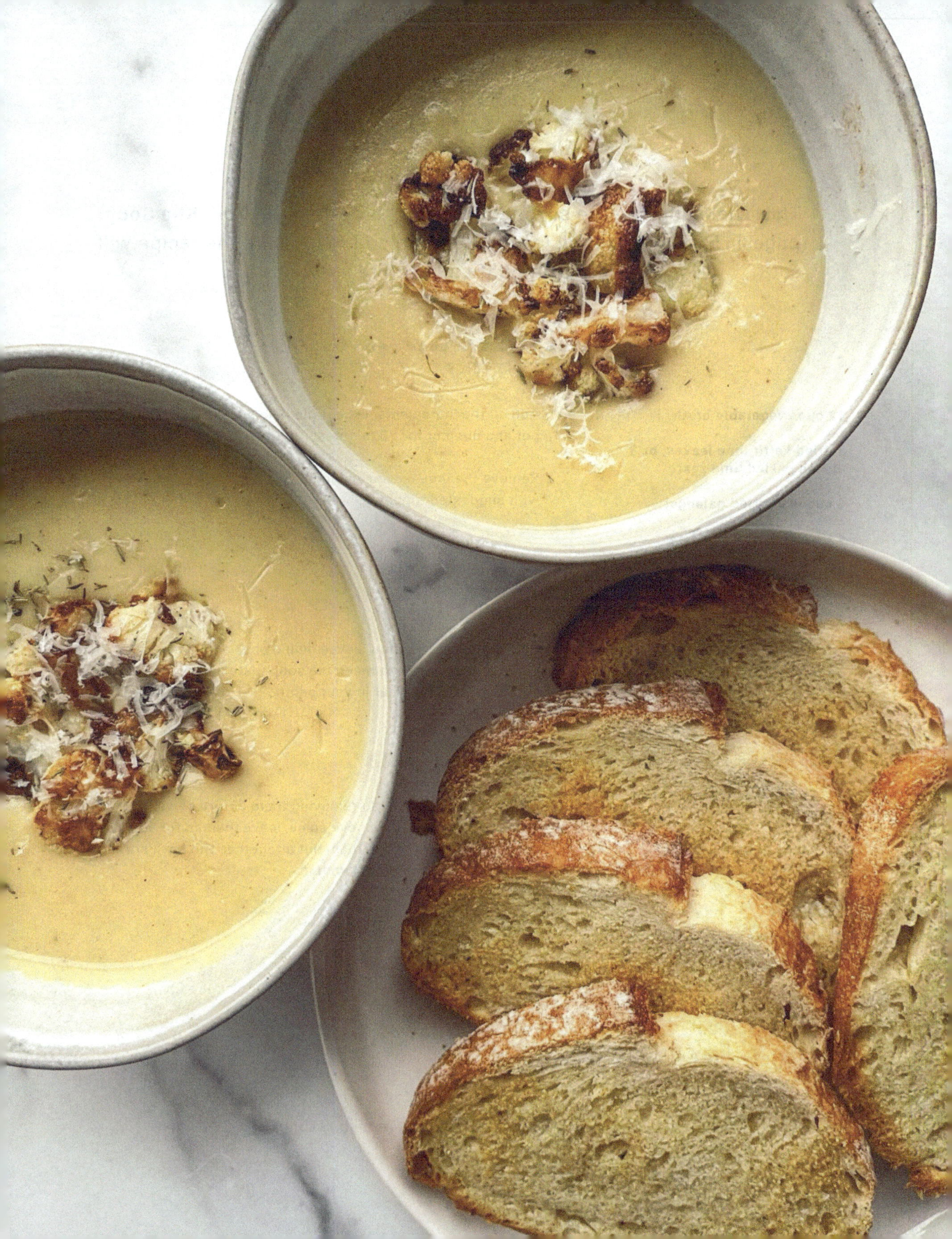

Tom Yum Soup

This Thai soup is more savory, sour, and spicy than the **Tom Kha Soup** (page 115). I know not all love spicy heat, so I made sure the recipe will accommodate all preferences.

SERVES 6, 1 1/2 cups per serving

12 cups vegetable broth

8 dried kaffir lime leaves, or 3 pieces peeled lime zest

6 slices of dried galangal

1 tbsp lemongrass paste

1 tbsp ginger paste

1 cup medium diced Roma tomatoes

1 ½ cups sliced mushrooms

14 oz container of extra firm tofu, diced in 1-inch pieces

½ white onion, sliced

3 tbsp soy sauce or liquid aminos

1 - 5 whole small dried Thai chili peppers

2 - 3 tbsp of lime juice (1 - 2 limes)
Salt to taste

Toppings
Chopped green onions and cilantro

Add all the ingredients, except the lime juice and toppings, to a pot and simmer for 30 minutes.

Remove the lime leaves, galangal, and chilies before serving with suggested toppings.

PRODUCT TIP

You can find kaffir lime leaves online or at an Asian foods market. They really do make the soup taste authentic. The dried variety will last all year in your pantry.

COOKING TIP

Thai chilies are spicy, so removing them before serving cuts the heat significantly. If you love spice, leave them in for serving. If you don't, you can leave them out altogether and have sriracha on the side for those who want it.

Calories 189 | Carbs 20g | Fat 3g | Protein 17g | Fiber 2g | Sodium 315mg

Tom Kha Soup (Coconut Soup)

Rich and delicious warm coconut soup. What could be better? Change up the proteins and veggies to be whatever your family likes.

SERVES 6, 1 1/2 cups per serving

¼ of white onion, sliced

½ of red bell pepper, sliced thin

6 slices of fresh ginger

2 stalks of lemongrass, scored down the center or 2 tbsp lemongrass paste

2 cups baby portabella or white button mushrooms, thinly sliced

2 cloves fresh garlic, sliced

14 oz package of firm tofu, drained and cubed

3 (13.5 oz) cans of Thai coconut milk

3 tbsp light soy sauce

1 tbsp sriracha

1 cup water

1 ½ tbsp coconut sugar or brown sugar

1 cup green cabbage, finely shredded

2 tbsp fresh lime juice

Toppings
Fresh cilantro, green onion, and Thai basil

Set a large soup pot to medium heat. Add all the ingredients through coconut sugar to the pot. Bring to a boil, then let simmer and cook for 10 minutes.

Add cabbage and cook for an additional 2 minutes. Add lime juice, turn off heat, and remove lemongrass and ginger pieces before serving. Top with suggested toppings.

🛒 PRODUCT TIP

The best authentic Thai canned coconut milk that I have found and love is called Chaokoh. Find it online or at some restaurant supply stores.

Calories 217 | Carbs 13g | Fat 15g | Protein 8g | Fiber 2g | Sodium 60mg

Red Pozole

Hands down my daughter's most requested recipe. She is obsessed with her mamma's pozole recipe.

SERVES 6, 1 1/2 cups per serving

1 medium sweet onion, diced

4 cloves fresh garlic, sliced

6 dried guajillo chili pods, stem and seeds removed

2 California or ancho chili pods, stem and seeds removed

2 Roma tomatoes, cut in chunks

1/2 tbsp Mexican oregano

2 tsp ground cumin

1/2 tbsp ground chili powder

7 cups low-sodium vegetable broth, divided

2 bay leaves

15 oz can pinto beans, drained and rinsed

15 oz can kidney beans, drained and rinsed

25 oz can hominy, drained and rinsed

1/2 tsp salt or to taste

Toppings

Thinly sliced radish, thinly sliced green cabbage, Mexican oregano, minced sweet onion, Tapatio or other hot sauce, lime wedges, chopped cilantro, corn tortilla chips or tostadas

Add the onion, garlic, both chilies, tomato, oregano, cumin, chili powder, and 2 cups of broth to a large soup pot. Simmer for 10 minutes. Carefully transfer to a blender and blend until smooth.

Add back to the pot with the remaining ingredients. Simmer for 25 minutes.

Remove the bay leaves and serve with toppings of choice.

MODIFICATION TIPS

I like blending the onions and garlic for this recipe to make it more kid-friendly. But if you prefer them visible, you can leave them out of blending and add during the second step. You will still need to cook the tomato and chilies before blending.

Feel free to add a pre-cooked protein of choice when serving up the soup. Something chopped or shredded that is already warmed works best.

Soup only
Calories 148 | Carbs 30g | Fat 1g | Protein 6g | Fiber 7g | Sodium 885mg

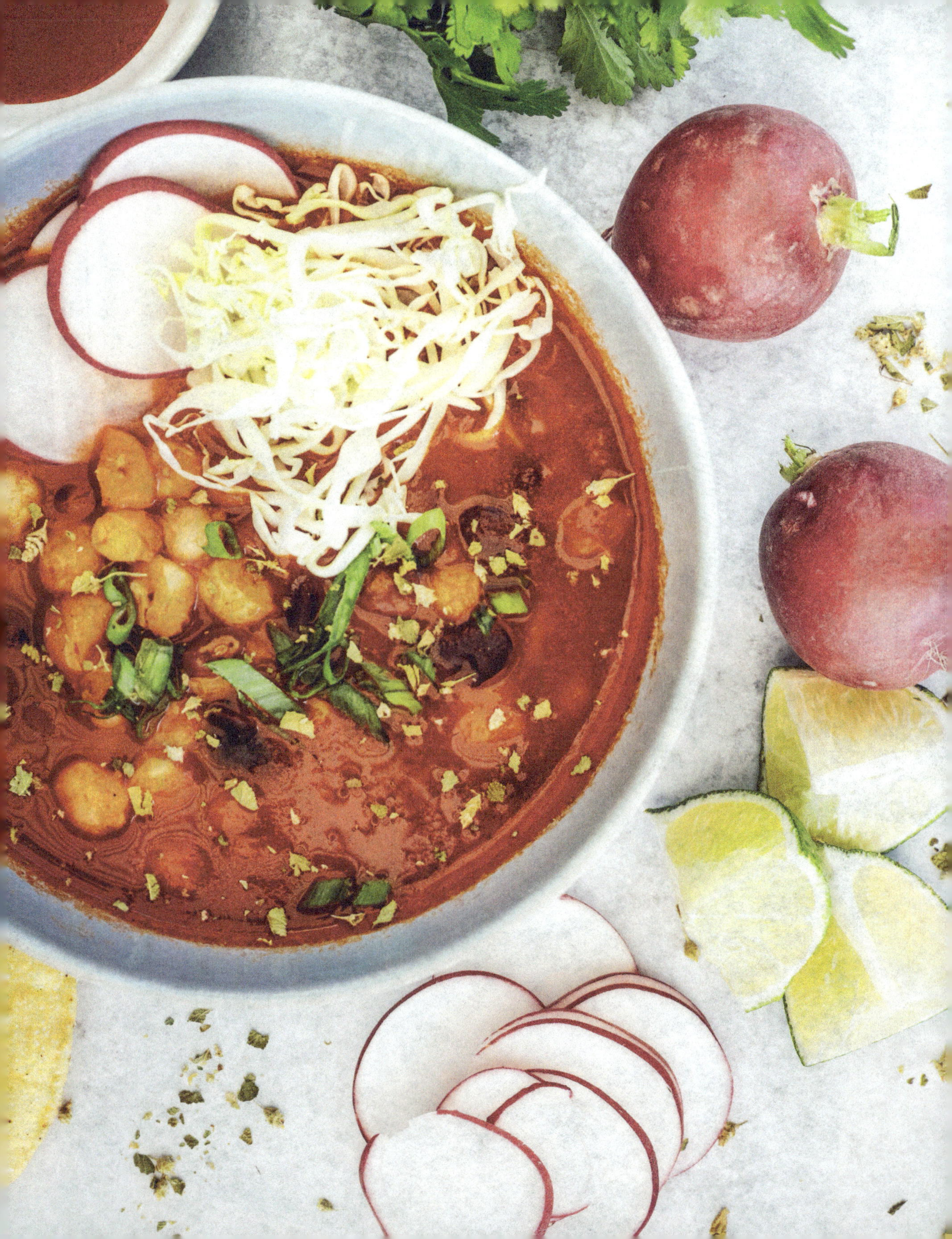

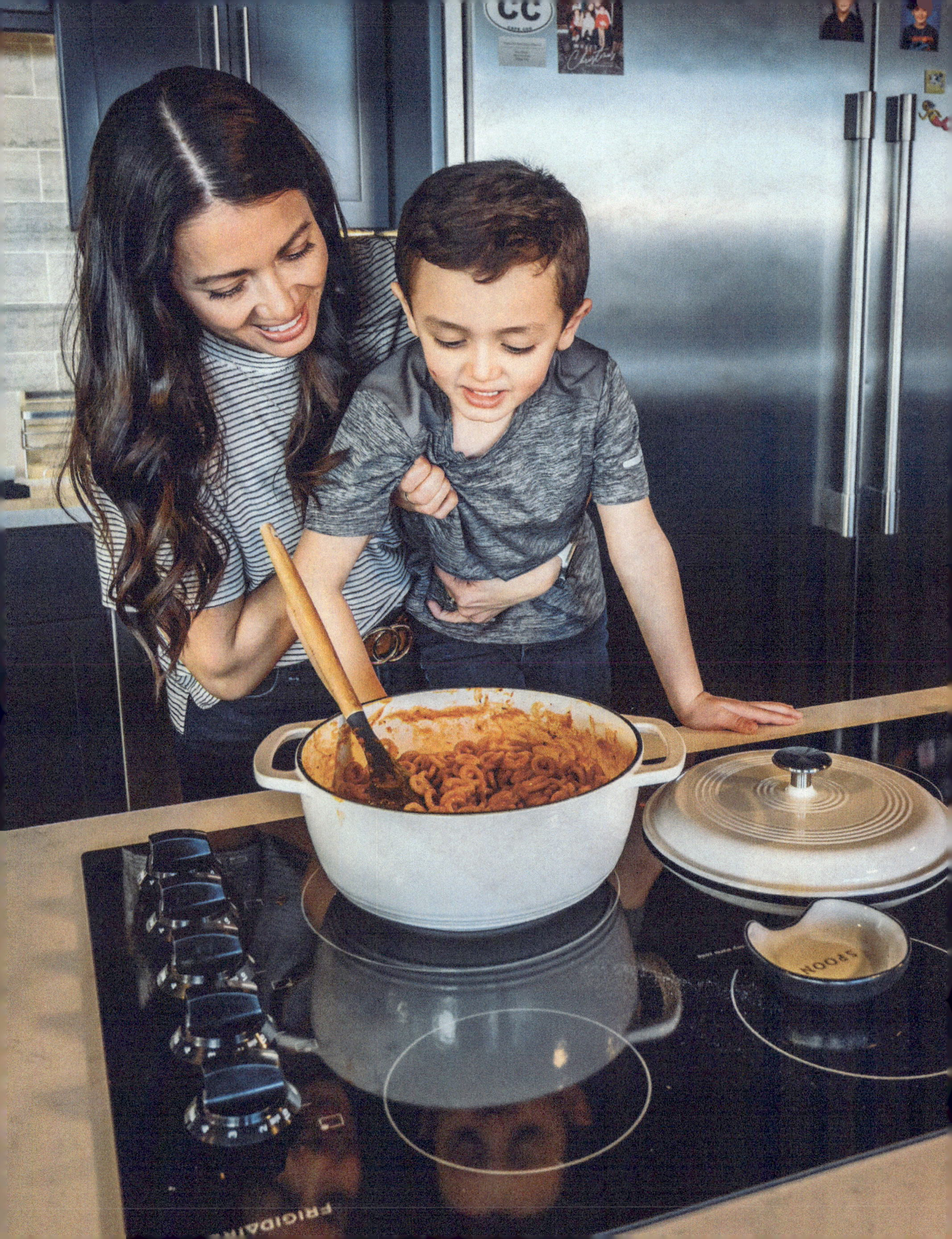
CC
SPOON
FRIGIDAIRE

Entrée Pastas

Thai Red Curry Noodles	**120**
Butternut Squash Lasagna Rolls	**123**
Spaghetti O's	**124**
Butternut Mac 'N Cheese	**127**
Baked Pumpkin Alfredo Pasta	**128**
Rainbow Pad Thai	**130**
Roasted Butternut Squash and Kale Pasta	**131**
Loaded Veggie Spaghetti Sauce	**132**

Thai Red Curry Noodles

These red curry noodles are a great way for kids to try curry. This recipe uses less curry paste, to reduce the heat, while adding paprika to retain the vibrant red color. Serve over noodles, rice, or another grain base.

SERVES 6, 3/4 cup per serving

- 1/2 tbsp neutral oil
- 1/2 medium white onion, sliced
- 2 tbsp minced fresh ginger or 1 tbsp ginger paste (if using paste, add to sauce mixture)
- 2 - 3 tbsp Thai red curry paste
- 2 tsp sweet paprika
- 2 tbsp minced garlic
- 1/4 cup coconut aminos
- 1 tbsp tamari or soy sauce
- 1 tbsp coconut sugar or maple syrup
- 2 dried kaffir lime leaves or 3 (2-inch) pieces of peeled lime
- 1 medium sweet potato or yam, peeled and diced into 1-inch pieces
- 2 (13.5 oz) cans Thai coconut milk*
- 13.5 oz can chickpeas, drained and rinsed
- 1 cup halved sugar snap peas
- Salt to taste

Serving and Toppings

- 8 oz package of thin rice noodles, brown rice, or cauliflower rice
- Chopped roasted peanuts, julienned or sliced Thai basil, chopped cilantro, and lime wedges

Add the oil to a deep skillet preheated to medium heat. Add the onion and ginger and sauté for 3 minutes.

Meanwhile, combine the curry paste, paprika, garlic, coconut aminos, liquid aminos or soy sauce, and sugar in a small bowl.

Add the kaffir lime leaves or lime peel, sweet potato or yam, coconut milk, chickpeas, curry sauce mixture, and water to the skillet and bring to a simmer. Cook for 15 minutes or until the sauce has thickened and sweet potato is fork-tender.

Add the snap peas and cook for another minute. Add salt as needed. Remove the kaffir lime leaves or lime peels and serve with rice base, peanuts, and topping suggestions.

PRODUCT TIPS

*Look for canned coconut milk made in Thailand. Those tend to have the best flavor for curry. I really like the Chaokoh brand.

Dried kaffir lime leaves can be purchased online and add a wonderful flavor to curry recipes. If you don't have any, you can use the peel of one whole lime instead. Just make sure to remove it before eating.

MODIFICATION TIPS

The snap peas can be steamed and on the side for those who prefer foods unmixed.

For kids that don't like pieces of onion and garlic in the curry, you can remove them after sautéing in step one and blend them into the coconut milk. Use the blended coconut milk mixture in the third step as directed in the instructions.

Curry only
Calories 321 | Carbs 35g | Fat 18g | Protein 6g | Fiber 5g | Sodium 100mg

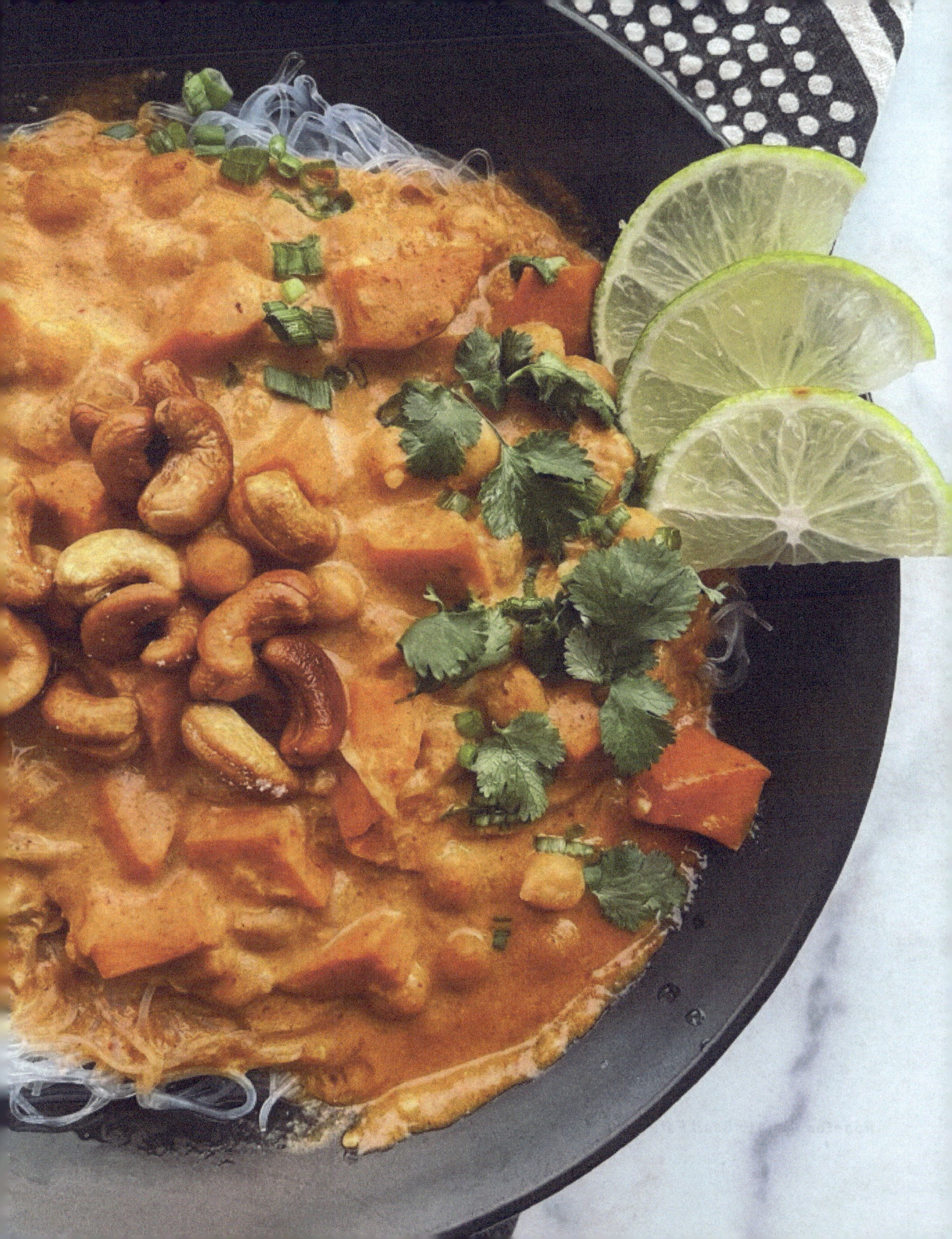

Roasted Tomato Basil Feta Soup (page 111)

Butternut Squash Lasagna Rolls

This version of lasagna is a great way to feed a crowd or just a hungry family. Serve with a big salad and you have a delicious and easy lasagna dinner!

MAKES 9, 1 roll per serving

Butternut Squash Sauce

1 lb butternut squash, peeled and diced into 1-inch pieces

1 tsp extra virgin olive oil

1/4 cup shallots, minced

4 cloves garlic, minced

1 cup unsweetened plain dairy-free or regular milk

1/4 tsp ground nutmeg

Salt and pepper to taste

Filling

15 oz dairy-free or regular low-fat ricotta cheese

10 oz frozen spinach or kale, defrosted and squeezed of most liquid

2 tbsp dairy-free or regular Parmesan

1 tbsp minced garlic

Pinch of salt and pepper

Lasagna and Topping

9 lasagna sheets, cooked to package instructions

3/4 cup panko breadcrumbs

4 tbsp dairy-free or regular Parmesan

1 tbsp extra virgin olive oil

1 tbsp fresh chopped parsley, plus some extra for serving

To make the sauce, boil the butternut squash until soft. Drain the squash and transfer to a blender. In a large deep non-stick skillet, add the oil and sauté the shallots and garlic over medium-low heat until soft, about 4–5 minutes. Add the sauteed shallots and garlic to the squash in the blender, along with the milk, nutmeg, salt, and pepper. Blend until smooth.

To make the topping, stir together the breadcrumbs, Parmesan, olive oil, and parsley.

Preheat oven to 350 degrees. Ladle about 1/2 cup butternut sauce on the bottom of a 9x13 baking dish.

For the filling, combine ricotta, spinach, Parmesan, garlic, salt, and pepper in a medium bowl.

To assemble, place a piece of wax paper on the counter and lay out lasagna noodles. Take 1/3 cup of ricotta mixture and spread evenly over each noodle. Roll and place seam side down onto the baking dish. Repeat with remaining noodles. Ladle about 1 cup of sauce over the noodles in the baking dish and top each roll with 1 heaping tablespoon of breadcrumb topping.

Bake for 25–30 minutes or until breadcrumbs are golden and rolls are heated through. Ladle a little extra sauce on each plate and top with lasagna roll. Garnish with extra parsley and serve.

MODIFICATION TIP

You can use a frozen cubed butternut squash instead of fresh. Just skip the boiling and add the defrosted squash directly to the blender. Continue with the rest of the instructions as written.

Calories 226 | Carbs 35g | Fat 4g | Protein 13g | Fiber 3g | Sodium 300mg

Spaghetti O's

I wanted to make a homemade version of the canned Spaghetti O's to share how easy it is to make them yourself. This recipe has so much more flavor and my daughter prefers this version over the canned.

SERVES 6, 3/4 cup per serving

8 oz anellini pasta, cooked until just tender, unrinsed after cooking

2 tbsp butter of choice

1 tbsp olive oil

1 tbsp garlic paste or pre-minced garlic

15 oz can tomato sauce

2 1/2 tbsp tomato paste

1/2 cup grated dairy-free or regular Parmesan

1 tsp sweet paprika

1 1/2 tsp onion powder

2 tbsp nutritional yeast, optional

2 cups water or broth of choice

Heat a medium pot to medium-low heat. Add the butter, oil, and garlic and sauté for 1 minute. Add the rest of the ingredients, except the pasta, and bring to a low simmer. Cook for 2–3 minutes or until sauce has reduced some and thickened, stirring often.

Add the pasta back to the pot and simmer in the sauce for 8–10 minutes until thickened, less time for gluten-free. It will continue to thicken and coat the pasta as it cools. Remove from heat and serve.

MODIFICATION TIP

You can use another small or round pasta such as alphabet pasta or rotelle (wagon wheel pasta) in place of the anellini. If your pasta is smaller, simmer the sauce longer to thicken, about 8–10 minutes total, then coat the pasta with the sauce. This also applies to gluten-free which tends to break down with too much cooking.

Calories 263 | Carbs 35g | Fat 8g | Protein 8g | Fiber 2g | Sodium 407mg

Entrée Pastas

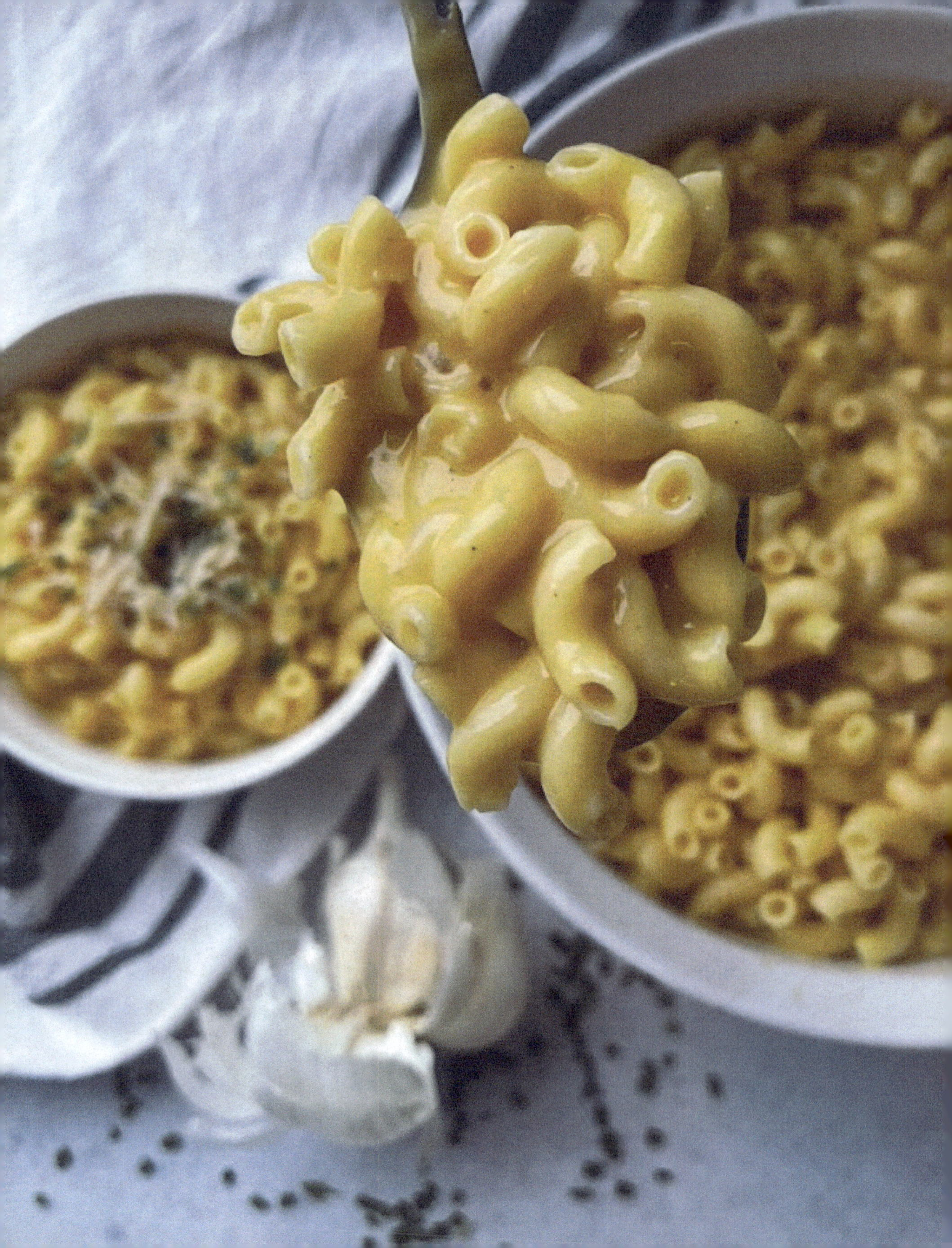

Butternut Mac 'N Cheese

I LOVE this version of mac 'n cheese. I have about five different recipes for mac 'n cheese, but I love how the squash gives this recipe even more of that authentic cheesy taste without tasting much of the squash. It's perfect for sneaking in those veggies.

SERVES 10, 1 cup per serving

2 cups medium diced butternut squash

3 cloves fresh garlic, left whole

1 medium shallot, roughly chopped

7 oz dairy-free or regular cheddar cheese, shredded or diced

5 oz dairy-free or regular Parmesan, grated or diced

1 cup vegetable broth

1 ½ cups unsweetened plain dairy-free or regular milk, homemade cashew milk works great

2 tbsp butter of choice

Salt and pepper to taste

12 oz elbow macaroni, cooked according to package instructions

Toppings
Chopped fresh parsley or chives and extra shredded dairy-free or regular Parmesan

Add the butternut squash, garlic, and shallot to a small pot. Cover with water, bring to a boil, and cook until squash is fork-tender, about 8–10 minutes. Drain mixture.

In a high-powered blender add the squash mixture, cheeses, broth, and milk. Blend until sauce is very smooth. Season with salt and pepper to taste.

Return pot to stove and set to medium heat. Add the butter and cheese sauce. Heat for about 3–5 minutes stirring frequently. Add the pasta and toss to coat. Remove from the heat and serve.

MODIFICATION TIP

You can use a frozen cubed butternut squash instead of fresh. Skip the boiling of the squash and add to the blender. Continue with the rest of the instructions as written.

Calories 325 | Carbs 13g | Fat 13g | Protein 13g | Fiber 3g | Sodium 505mg

Baked Pumpkin Alfredo Pasta

I love pumpkin recipes and not just for fall and winter. When used in smaller amounts, pumpkin can add creaminess to recipes without an overpowering flavor. Everything is cooked in the oven here, even the pasta. This weeknight meal is so hands-off and easy; it will become your new go-to pasta!

SERVES 6, 1 cup per serving

3 cups or 8 oz medium shell pasta or any short pasta

½ cup pumpkin puree

2 tbsp minced garlic

3 cups vegetable broth

½ cup whole raw cashews, soaked for 4 hours, then drained

1 cup water

⅓ cup grated or shredded dairy-free or regular Parmesan

1 tsp white or yellow miso paste

2 tbsp butter of choice

Salt and pepper to taste

Toppings
Chopped fresh sage and more dairy-free or regular Parmesan

Preheat the oven to 350 degrees. In a Dutch oven or other baking dish with a lid, add the pasta, pumpkin, garlic, and broth. Mix well, making sure the pasta is completely submerged. Cover and bake for 30–35 minutes or until tender.

While pasta is baking, add the cashews, water, Parmesan, and miso paste to a high-powered blender and blend until very smooth. Salt and pepper to taste.

Once the pasta is cooked, add the cashew mixture and butter, then mix together well. Pasta sauce will thicken as it sits. Add more water or broth as needed. Season with salt and pepper to taste and top with fresh chopped sage and Parmesan.

PRODUCT TIP

Miso paste can be found in the produce section of most grocery stores. Try to use a white or yellow paste to keep the color neutral and not change the final color of the pasta.

COOKING TIP

Gluten-free pasta works well for this recipe. Make sure to use a short cut pasta and check for doneness. The great thing about cooking gluten-free pasta like this is it doesn't fall apart as easily as using the boiling method.

Calories 297 | Carbs 38g | Fat 13g | Protein 6g | Fiber 2g | Sodium 325mg

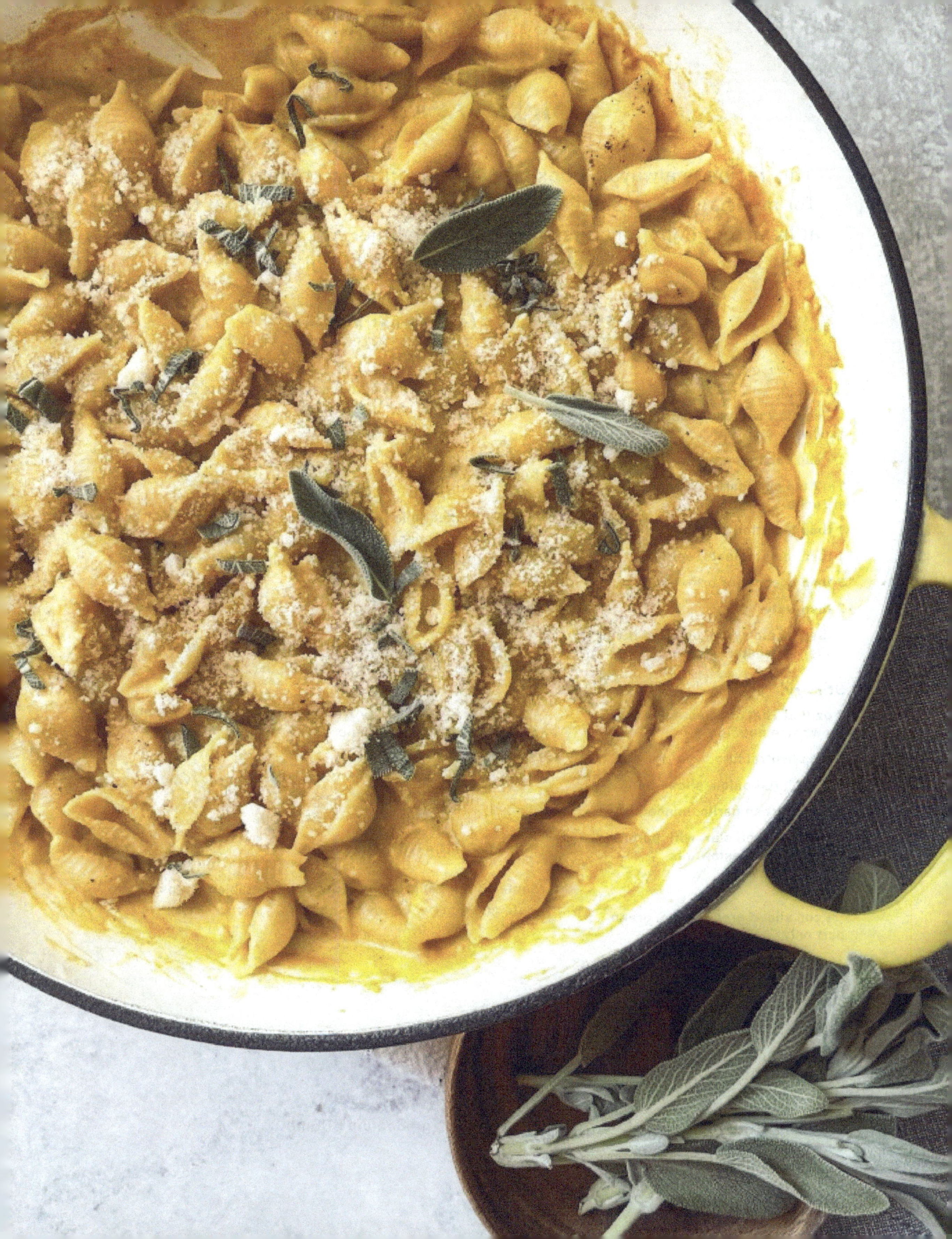

Rainbow Pad Thai

This recipe is always a cooking class favorite for students. Many sign up for my Thai One class because of Pad Thai. It can be difficult to recreate at home but hopefully this gives you a healthier, yet authentic, version you feel good about serving often!

SERVES 5, 1 1/4 cups per serving

Sauce
1/4 cup low sodium tamari or soy sauce

1/4 cup coconut aminos

1 - 2 tsp chili garlic sauce or sriracha

1 tbsp tamarind paste

1 tbsp tomato paste, optional

3 tbsp coconut or brown sugar

3 tbsp water

1 tbsp maple syrup, optional if you prefer it sweeter

Stir Fry
8 oz Pad Thai noodles, I like the brown rice noodles

3 tbsp neutral oil

1/2 small red onion, sliced thin

2 cloves fresh garlic, minced

2 cups broccoli slaw with purple cabbage or coleslaw mix

Toppings
1/3 cup sliced green onion, green part only

1/3 cup chopped cilantro

12 oz bag of mung bean sprouts or extra cabbage

1/3 cup ground peanuts

1 lime, cut into 4 wedges

In a small bowl, whisk all the sauce ingredients together and set aside.

Soak the noodles in a large casserole dish with boiling water for 10 minutes.

Meanwhile, heat a large skillet to medium heat. Add oil, onion, garlic, and slaw package to skillet and sauté for 5–6 minutes. Drain the noodles and add to the skillet with the veggies and stir fry for 2 minutes.

Add the sauce and stir fry again for another 2 minutes or until most of the sauce is absorbed and the noodles are tender. Toss lightly when cooking to not break up the noodles.

Divide into bowls and top with green onion, cilantro, mung bean sprouts, peanuts, and a lime wedge.

MODIFICATION TIP

Sauté additional protein before the vegetables. Transfer to a plate and add back with the noodles.

Calories 382 | Carbs 70g | Fat 8g | Protein 9g | Fiber 7g | Sodium 500mg

Roasted Butternut Squash and Kale Pasta

In the fall and winter, squash is everywhere. It's hard to keep it interesting, but this recipe is a nice change from the average. Both the squash and the kale are roasted in the oven, giving a caramelized, toasted flavor to both veggies. This no-sauce pasta is perfect for company or an at-home date night.

SERVES 2, 1/2 the pasta per serving

2 cups fresh large-diced butternut squash

1 tbsp extra virgin olive oil

1/2 tbsp fresh thyme leaves, stems removed

1/2 tsp dried sage leaves

1 cup torn or chopped kale, bite-sized pieces

1/2 cup vegetable broth*

1/2 tbsp minced garlic

6 oz bow tie pasta, cooked according to box instructions

2 tbsp extra virgin olive oil

Salt and fresh ground pepper to taste

Toppings

Red pepper flakes, dairy-free or regular Parmesan, thyme leaves, ground walnuts or pecans

Preheat the oven to 425 degrees and line a baking sheet with parchment paper. Toss the diced butternut squash with 1 tablespoon of olive oil, thyme, sage leaves, salt, and pepper in a bowl. Spread evenly onto a baking sheet and roast for 20 minutes.

Toss the kale in a little olive oil, about half a tablespoon, or what is left over from the squash in the bowl, and season with salt and pepper. Add the kale to the butternut squash and roast for another 3–4 minutes. Remove and set aside.

In a large skillet, add the broth and garlic. Simmer on medium heat for 2–3 minutes. Add the pasta, roasted squash and kale, and the 2 tablespoons of olive oil. Season with salt and pepper and toss well to combine everything. Plate and garnish with suggestions.

PRODUCT TIP

*I've said this before in other recipe tips, but I love broth pastes. They have way more flavor and add so much to a dish. Better Than Bouillon makes a No Chicken Base that I love; you can find it online or at some grocery stores.

Calories 250 | Carbs 30g | Fat 15g | Protein 4g | Fiber 4g | Sodium 400mg

Loaded Veggie Spaghetti Sauce

I've been making this spaghetti sauce for my daughter for years now and it is still a family favorite. Use it for anything, especially lasagna!

SERVES 8, 1/2 cup of sauce per serving

8 oz sliced mushrooms

1/2 red bell pepper, cut in chunks

1/2 medium sweet onion, cut in chunks

1 tbsp butter of choice

2 tbsp olive oil

1 cup frozen cauliflower rice

2 tbsp minced garlic

1/4 cup red cooking wine

1 tsp ground fennel, optional

2 tbsp Italian herb seasoning

24 oz jar marinara or pasta sauce

28 oz can crushed Italian herb tomatoes

1 cup water

Salt and pepper to taste

Garnish
Fresh chopped basil

Add the mushrooms, bell pepper, and onion to a food processor and pulse until desired size pieces. I prefer mine pretty small.

Turn the Instant Pot or electric pressure cooker on sauté. Add the butter, oil, mushroom mixture, and cauliflower rice and cook for 5–6 minutes. Add the garlic and cooking wine and cook another 5 minutes or until most of the liquid has evaporated.

Add the spices, marinara sauce, crushed tomatoes, and water to the pot. Press cancel, then set to high pressure for 5 minutes.

When done, manually or quick release the steam. Season with salt and pepper; garnish with basil. Serve over pasta of choice.

COOKING TIP

If you do not have an Instant Pot or electric pressure cooker, you can cook this sauce on the stove. Reduce the water to 1/2 cup and follow the instructions using a medium pot. Simmer on medium-low for 25–30 minutes, stirring frequently.

MODIFICATION TIP

You can change some of the vegetables, either by leaving them out or replacing with another option. Just make sure that the vegetables blend into the sauce as either something that resembles meat or looks like the tomato sauce and can be cooked without becoming mushy.

Calories 141 | Carbs 14g | Fat 6g | Protein 5g | Fiber 2g | Sodium 437mg

Entrée Pastas

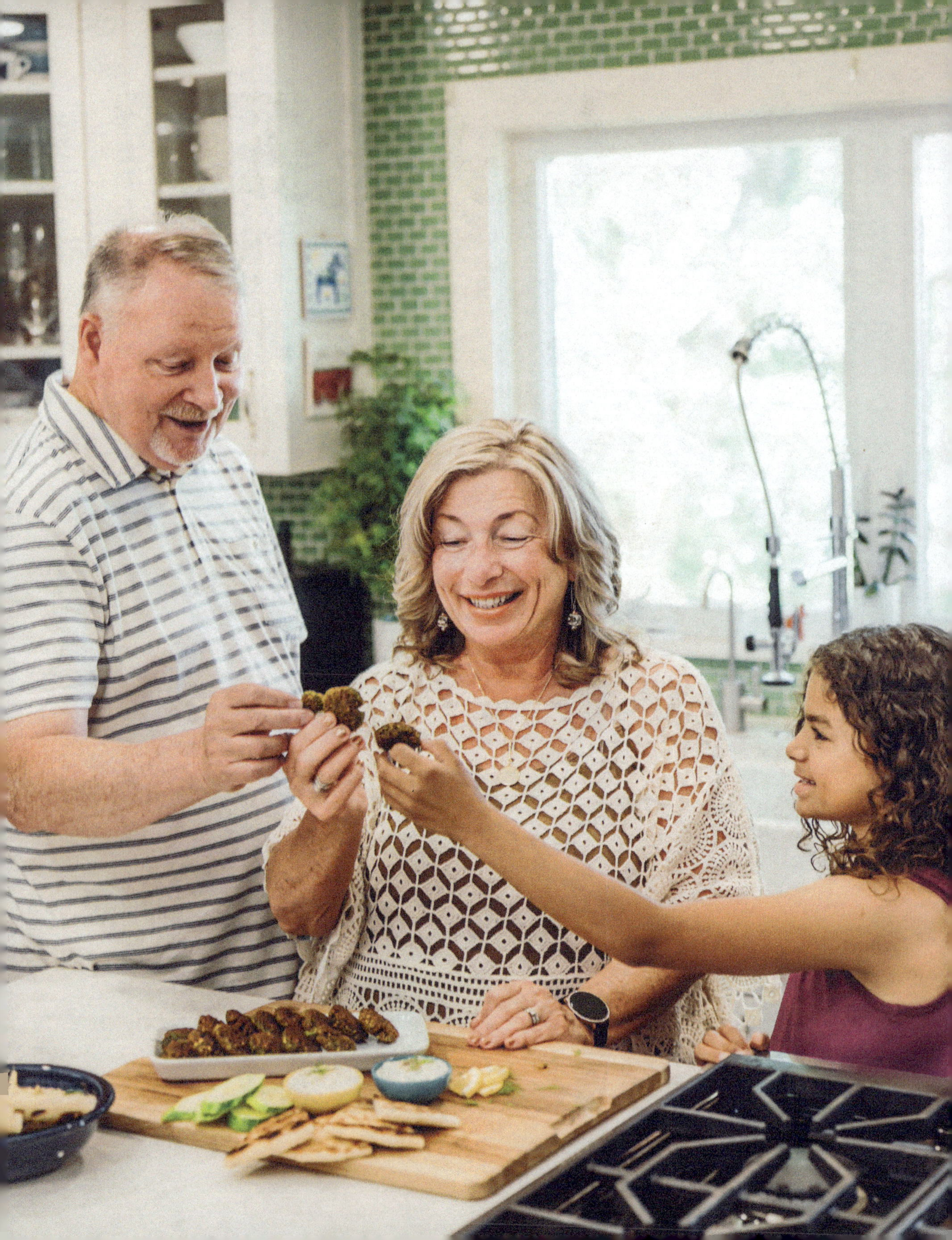

Beans and Lentils

Southern Instant Pot Red Beans	**136**
Cheesy Socca Pizza	**138**
Indian Chickpea Chana Masala	**141**
Instant Pot "Refried" Pink Beans	**142**
Mixed Veggie Pakoras	**143**
Falafels with Tzatziki Sauce	**144**
Pumpkin Sweet Potato Chili	**147**
Deli Chick'n Chickpea Salad	**148**
Greek Lentil Soup "Fakes"	**150**
Lentil Meatballs	**151**

Southern Instant Pot Red Beans

I grew up in Alabama loving Red Beans and Rice. This is my take on that traditional dish. Serve over brown rice and add a salad or southern-inspired vegetables on the side for a complete meatless Monday meal.

SERVES 4, 1 cup per serving

2 tbsp neutral oil

1/2 sweet onion, diced small

1 stalk of celery, diced small

1/2 red bell pepper, diced small

1 tbsp minced garlic

2 (15.5 oz) cans dark red kidney beans, drained

1 cup vegetable stock

1/2 tsp dried thyme

1/2 tsp dried oregano

1/2 tsp celery salt

1/2 tbsp paprika

1/2 tsp hickory liquid smoke

Salt and pepper to taste

Serving and Topping Options
Cooked brown or white rice

Chopped green onions

Turn the Instant Pot or electric pressure cooker on medium sauté and add the oil, onion, celery, and bell pepper and sauté for 5 minutes. Add the rest of the ingredients.

Turn off the Instant Pot and set to high pressure for 12 minutes.

Once the cooking is done, cover the vent with a towel and release the pressure. Use a potato masher to break up some of the beans.

Season with salt and pepper. Serve with brown or white rice and green onions.

MODIFICATION TIP

If your family doesn't like pieces of vegetables, sauté the onion, celery, and bell pepper, then blend with the broth until smooth. Combine with the rest of the ingredients and continue with the instructions.

Calories 161 | Carbs 18g | Fat 7g | Protein 6g | Fiber 7g | Sodium 124mg

THE ORIGINAL
"LOUISIANA"
THE PERFECT
HOT SAUCE
ONE DROP DOES IT

Cheesy Socca Pizza

Socca is a Mediterranean garbanzo bean flour bread high in fiber and protein. The batter is super simple with just a few ingredients. Cook in a skillet like a big pancake, top with your favorite pizza toppings, and bake. You are going to love how filling and good-for-you this pizza is!

SERVES 2, 1/2 the pizza per serving

½ cup ground chickpea flour

½ cup hot tap water

1 tbsp extra virgin or light olive oil

½ tbsp Italian herb seasoning

¼ tsp salt

1 tbsp neutral oil

⅓ cup marinara or pizza sauce of choice

¼ cup shredded dairy-free or regular mozzarella

Whisk together the flour, water, 1 tablespoon of olive oil, Italian seasoning, and salt in a medium bowl. Let batter rest for at least 30 minutes or up to 6 hours.

Preheat a 10-inch non-stick skillet to medium heat. Once hot, drizzle with 1 tbsp of neutral oil and coat the bottom of the skillet. Pour the batter into a ¼-inch thick round, even layer at the bottom of the skillet. It is good to have a gap between the edge of the batter and the rim of the skillet for easier flipping.

Cook for 3–4 minutes. Socca should be crisp, golden, and set on the cooked side. Flip and cook again for 3 minutes. Transfer to a parchment-lined baking sheet.

Preheat the oven to 500 degrees. Top socca crust with sauce and cheese. Bake for 8–10 minutes.

Remove from oven. Cool for 5 minutes, then cut into 4 pieces.

COOKING TIP

When pouring the batter into the skillet, try doing it in one even pass around the pan. Adding more batter to the edges might cause the socca to break. Use a wide spatula to flip the socca in the skillet.

Calories 279 | Carbs 25g | Fat 14g | Protein 12g | Fiber 7g | Sodium 642mg

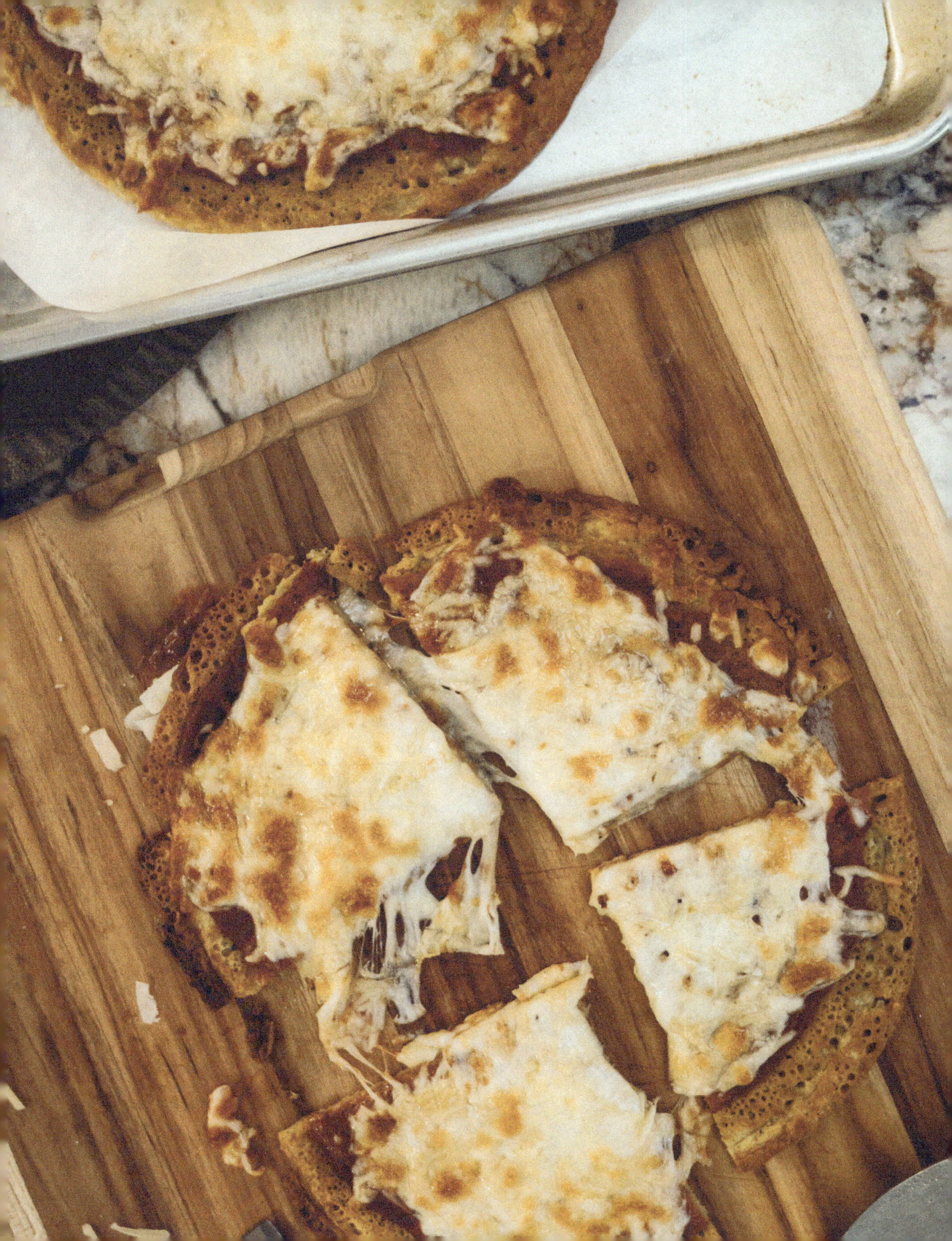

Cheesy Socca Pizza (page 138)

Indian Chickpea Chana Masala

I love this dish for many reasons, but mostly because it uses common pantry ingredients. Have these staple Indian spices on hand and a few canned items and you're good to go!

SERVES 4, 1 cup per serving

1 tsp neutral oil

1/2 white or sweet onion, diced

15 oz can petite diced tomatoes

2 (15 oz) cans chickpeas, drained and rinsed

13.5 oz can light coconut milk

1 tbsp ginger paste or fresh minced ginger

1 tbsp minced garlic

1/4 tsp ground cinnamon

1 tsp ground coriander

1/2 tsp ground cardamom

2 tsp ground cumin

3 tsp garam masala

Salt to taste

Rice or quinoa for serving

Garnish

Plain yogurt and chopped fresh cilantro

Heat a large skillet to medium and add oil. Add the onion and cook for 2 minutes, stirring frequently.

Add the rest of the ingredients except the garnish, then cover and simmer for 15 minutes. Uncover and simmer for another 10–15 minutes or until sauce reduces slightly.

Serve over rice, quinoa, or on its own. Top with plain yogurt and cilantro.

MODIFICATION TIP

For those who don't like chunks of tomato and onion, blend the onions and tomatoes with the coconut milk after the onions are sautéed. Add to the skillet with the rest of the ingredients and cook as instructed.

Calories 324 | Carbs 39g | Fat 14g | Protein 11g | Fiber 9g | Sodium 300mg

Instant Pot "Refried" Pink Beans

One of my clients told me about using pink beans for refried beans. They are creamier and sweeter than pinto beans and more of a traditional bean. I tried them and fell in love!

MAKES 10 SERVINGS, 1/2 cup per serving

1 lb dried pinto or pink beans, soaked 12–24 hours, then drained

2 tbsp neutral oil

1 small sweet onion, diced

4 cloves fresh garlic, chopped

3 cups of water

1 tbsp ground cumin

1 tbsp dried oregano

1 tsp granulated sugar, optional

1 1/2 - 2 tsp salt

Salt and pepper to taste

Topping Options
Chopped cilantro, crumbled Cotija cheese, and minced yellow or red onion

Heat the Instant Pot or electric pressure cooker to medium in the sauté function. Add the oil, onion, garlic, and cook for 5 minutes. Add the water and beans.

Turn the Instant Pot off then switch to manual high pressure for 20 minutes. Once done, use the manual release to release the lid. Check four or six beans for tenderness. Add more cooking time if needed. Add the rest of the ingredients to the beans.

Use a potato masher or an immersion blender to make the beans creamy to desired texture.

Portion and garnish with option suggestions. If using for enchiladas, cool completely for thicker beans.

COOKING TIP

When cooking dry soaked or unsoaked beans, don't salt the water. Salt slows the cooking process down. Salt the beans after they are tender. Always check at least six beans for tenderness as some may need more time to cook than others.

Without toppings
Calories 170 | Carbs 28g | Fat 4g | Protein 9g | Fiber 7g | Sodium 400mg

Mixed Veggie Pakoras

I love Indian Pakoras. Crispy and so full of flavor, they are a great way to make vegetables taste great! Serve with your favorite Indian chutney recipe or check out the two chutney recipes in my first cookbook, *Cooking Healthy!*

SERVES 8, 3/4 cup per serving

2 cups chickpea flour

1 tsp baking powder

1 1/2 tsp cumin seeds

1 tbsp garam or chaat masala

1 tsp ground turmeric

1/4 cup chopped cilantro

3/4 tsp salt

1 1/2 cups water (add more if too thick)

1/2 - 1 whole medium jalapeno, seeds removed and diced small, optional

3 cups veggies of choice, cut into 1 - 1 1/2-inch pieces (potato, onion, cauliflower, broccoli, zucchini)

Neutral oil for pan frying (about 1/3 cup)

Heat a deep skillet to medium heat. In a bowl, add the chickpea flour, baking powder, cumin, masala, turmeric, cilantro, and salt and whisk together. Add the water and mix. Fold in the pieces of veggies until everything is well combined.

Add enough oil to lightly coat the bottom of the skillet. Once hot, add each veggie separately to the skillet, and don't overcrowd the pan. Cook each one for 3–4 minutes or until golden brown on each side.

Adjust the heat down if it gets too hot or cooks too fast. Drain each batch on a plate lined with paper towels and season with salt. Repeat until all the pakoras are done. Serve with chutney of choice.

COOKING TIP

Choose vegetables that can cook in a short amount of time and are cut in the recommended size above. Potatoes can definitely be used, but they need to be sliced 1/4-inch thick. Onions are my absolute favorite, but for kids, cauliflower works great.

Calories 218 | Carbs 23g | Fat 11g | Protein 7g | Fiber 6g | Sodium 167mg

Falafels with Tzatziki Sauce

These falafels are so flavorful and delicious. Herby, crispy, and perfect dipped in traditional **Tzatziki Sauce** (page 146) or **Herb Feta Dip** (page 49). You are going to love them on a salad or in addition to your favorite Greek or Mediterranean meal.

MAKES 30, 5 falafels per serving

1 cup dry garbanzo beans, soaked in water for 24 hours

½ medium white onion, coarsely chopped

4 cloves fresh garlic

1 cup packed flat leaf parsley

1 cup packed cilantro

2 tsp ground cumin

1 tsp ground coriander

¼ tsp red pepper flakes, optional

1 tsp salt

2 tbsp all-purpose gluten-free or regular flour

1 tsp baking powder

Cooking spray or neutral oil for frying

COOKING TIP

The falafel batter will feel a little wet but should hold together when pressed. Roll into a ball first, then press flat into a disk shape.

Drain the soaked chickpeas and place on a baking sheet with a drying cloth. Dry chickpeas well before using.

Add all the ingredients, except cooking spray and oil, to a food processor and pulse until mixture looks like a coarse sticky meal. Mixture should stick together when pressed between fingers. You may need to stop the processor occasionally and scrape the sides.

If dough seems too wet, add an additional 1 tablespoon of flour. Mixture should be a consistent coarse meal texture. Transfer to a mixing bowl. Mold the falafel mixture into 2-inch patties.

BAKING INSTRUCTIONS

Preheat the oven to 375 degrees. Line a baking sheet with parchment or a silicone baking mat. Spray the parchment and arrange the patties in rows, leaving space between them. Bake for 12–15 minutes on each side until each is golden and crisp. Cool and salt the tops.

FRYING INSTRUCTIONS

In a frying pan, heat a ½-inch deep layer of avocado or grapeseed oil to medium heat. When oil is hot or bubbles form around the end of a wooden spoon, gently lay half the patties in the pan and fry on each side for 2–3 minutes or until golden. Drain excess oil on a paper towel and salt the tops.

Tzatziki Sauce recipe on page 146...

Baked version
Calories 129 | Carbs 24g | Fat 2g | Protein 7g | Fiber 6g | Sodium 443mg

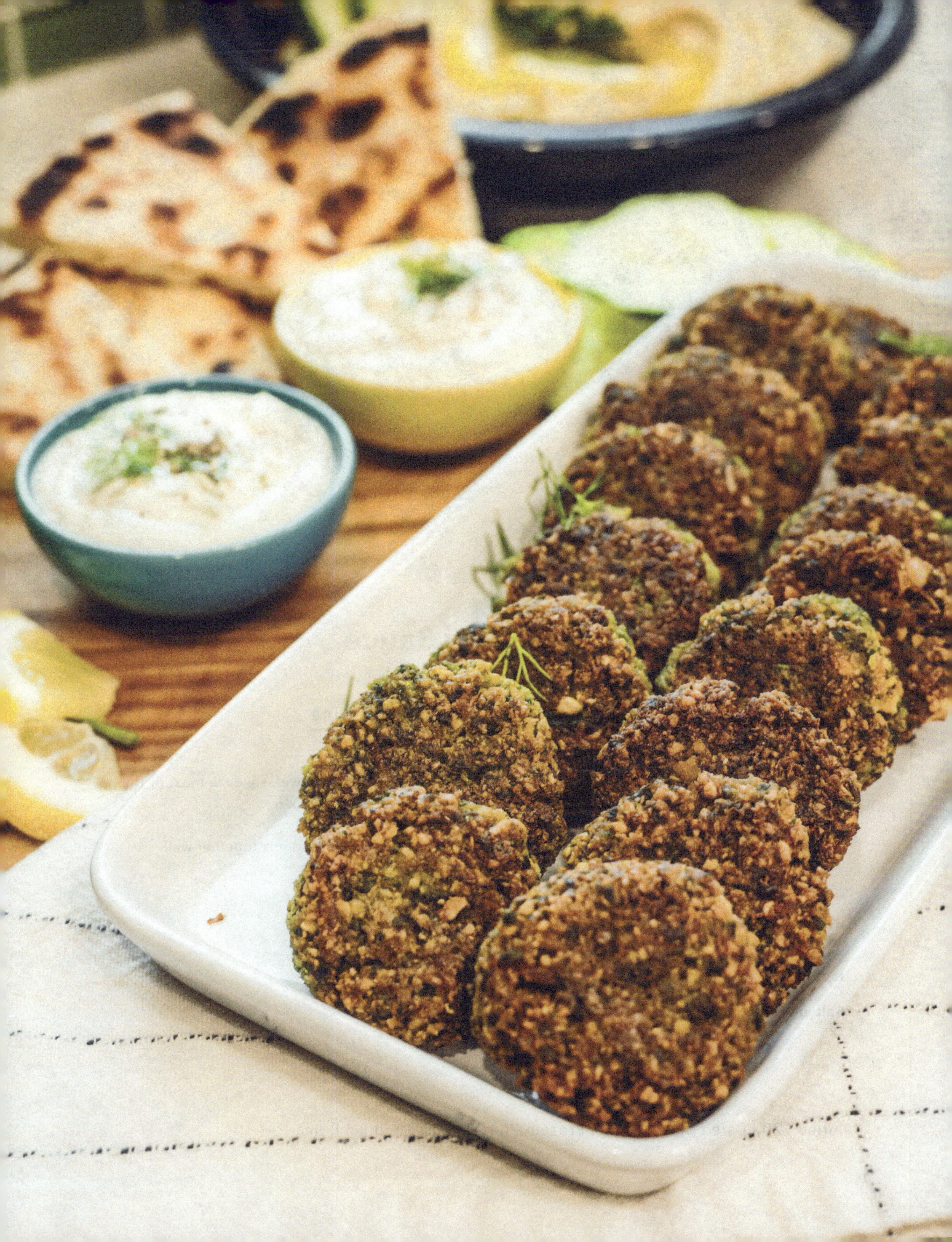

Herb Feta Dip (page 49)

Tzatziki Sauce

SERVES 6, 2 tbsp per serving

1 English cucumber, peeled, de-seeded, and shredded

10 oz or 1 1/4 cup dairy-free or regular plain yogurt

1/4 cup mayonnaise of choice

Juice of one lemon

2 tbsp finely chopped fresh dill or 2 tsp dry

Salt and pepper to taste

Using a kitchen towel or paper towel, squeeze most of the liquid out of the shredded cucumber.

Place all ingredients in a bowl and mix together well.

Calories 120 | Carbs 3g | Fat 10g | Protein 2g | Fiber 1g | Sodium 80mg

Pumpkin Sweet Potato Chili

Pumpkin and sweet potato are very similar in taste and texture. In this chili, we are using both, one pureed and other cubed. The protein and fiber are high, making this chili delicious and super nutritious!

SERVES 6, 1 cup per serving

2 (15.5 oz) cans pinto beans, only one drained

15.5 oz can black beans, rinsed and drained

1 cup pumpkin puree

2 tbsp light brown sugar

1 tbsp molasses

1 tbsp chili powder

1 tbsp Worcestershire sauce

1 tsp hickory liquid smoke

1 tsp ground cumin

1 tsp garlic powder

¼ tsp pumpkin pie spice

½ tsp chipotle chili powder, optional

4 cloves fresh garlic, minced

1 medium sweet potato, medium diced

1 cup water or broth

Salt to taste

Add all the ingredients to a soup pot. Heat chili over medium-high heat until simmering, then reduce to medium-low to maintain a low simmer.

Cook for 30 minutes with the lid on, stirring every 5 minutes to keep chili from sticking. Chili is done when it has thickened and sweet potatoes are fork-tender.

MODIFICATION TIP

Feel free to add another protein, but with 14 grams of protein per serving, this chili packs a lot already!

Calories 281 | Carbs 55g | Fat 1g | Protein 14g | Fiber 12g | Sodium 200mg

Deli Chick'n Chickpea Salad

Like many bean dishes, this quick version of a chicken salad is high in protein and fiber. Those complex carbohydrates will increase satiety and satisfaction.

SERVES 4, 1/2 cup per serving

- 15.5 oz can chickpeas, drained and rinsed
- 2 stalks celery, sliced
- 3 green onions, sliced
- 1/2 cup walnuts, coarsely chopped
- 1/2 cup green grapes, halved
- 3 tbsp mayonnaise of choice
- 1 tsp Dijon mustard
- 1 tsp dried dill
- 1/2 tsp poultry seasoning
- 1/2 tsp kosher salt
- 1/4 tsp fresh ground black pepper

In a medium bowl, add chickpeas and gently mash with potato masher or fork, leaving some beans whole. Add celery, green onion, walnuts, and grapes, and mix together.

In a small bowl, add mayo, Dijon, dill, poultry seasoning, salt, and pepper, and mix well.

Add dressing to the chickpea mixture and combine until evenly distributed. Taste and adjust seasoning as needed. The flavor is best if salad is made ahead of time, up to one day. Refrigerate until ready to serve.

Calories 250 | Carbs 33g | Fat 10g | Protein 10g | Fiber 9g | Sodium 448mg

Falafels with Tzatziki Sauce (page 144)

Greek Lentil Soup "Fakes"

This version of a traditional Greek Fakes soup packs a nice bright flavor with the addition of red wine vinegar and olive oil on top of each bowl.

SERVES 8, 1 cup per serving

1 medium sweet onion, diced small

2 medium carrots, diced small

2 stalks celery, diced small

1 tbsp minced garlic

1 1/2 cups dried green or brown lentils

3 dried bay leaves

1/2 tsp ground cumin

1 tsp dried oregano

14 oz can diced tomatoes

6 cups vegetable broth

Salt and pepper to taste

Garnish
Drizzle of red wine vinegar and/or good olive oil, shredded dairy-free or regular Parmesan

Add all the ingredients to an Instant Pot or electric pressure cooker, except the salt, pepper, and toppings. Turn the pressure cooker on manual high pressure for 14 minutes.

Manually release the steam. Season soup with salt and pepper to taste. Remove bay leaves and garnish with suggested toppings.

COOKING TIP

This soup can be made on the stove in a medium soup pot. Follow instructions but bring to a simmer and cook for 25–30 minutes.

Calories 221 | Carbs 28g | Fat 6g | Protein 12g | Fiber 13g | Sodium 290mg

Lentil Meatballs

I remember tricking my husband the first time he tried these—he totally thought they were meat! They are so good crisped up in an air fryer, but the oven works fine, too.

SERVES 4, 5 meatballs per person

½ tbsp neutral oil

8 oz container sliced portabella or cremini mushrooms

1 tbsp Italian herb seasoning

1 cup Italian breadcrumbs

1 tbsp minced garlic

1 tbsp dairy-free or regular Parmesan or nutritional yeast

1 tbsp fresh chopped parsley

1 ½ tbsp ketchup

1 tbsp extra virgin olive oil

1 ½ cups cooked brown or green lentils

Cooking spray

Heat a skillet to medium heat. Add oil and mushrooms. Cook for 5 minutes, stirring occasionally. In a mixing bowl, add the Italian seasoning, breadcrumbs, garlic, Parmesan or nutritional yeast, parsley, ketchup, and olive oil. Stir to combine.

Add the lentils and cooked mushrooms to a food processor and process until mostly smooth but still a little chunky, like a chunky paste. Add lentil mixture to the rest of the ingredients in the mixing bowl and combine mixture well. If too dry to stick together, add another tablespoon of olive oil or ketchup.

Spray the inside of the air fryer basket with cooking spray. Roll lentil mixture into twenty 1 ½-inch balls. Fill the basket with 6 - 8 balls, but do not overcrowd the basket.

Cook at 370 degrees for 12–14 minutes shaking the basket or flipping halfway through. Repeat the cooking process with the rest of the batches.

PRODUCT TIP

Cooking dried lentils isn't difficult, but I love having canned lentils on hand for quick meals. They work great in this recipe.

COOKING TIP

If using the oven, cook at 375 degrees for 20–22 minutes, turning halfway through.

Calories 277 | Carbs 35g | Fat 9g | Protein 11g | Fiber 8g | Sodium 24mg

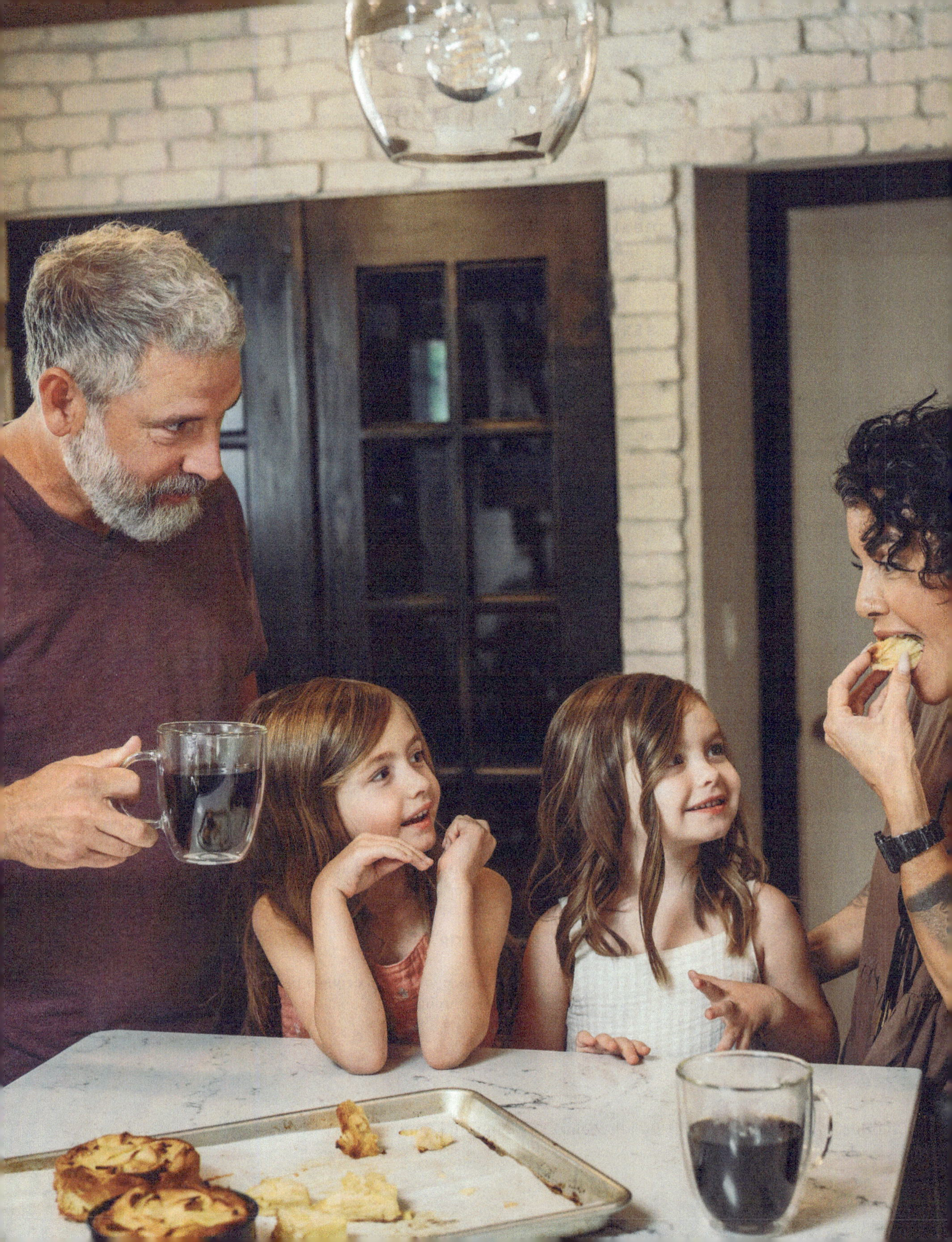

Sweet Treats

Haupia Coconut Pudding	**155**
Lemon Amaretti Cookies	**156**
Cranberry Orange Biscotti	**157**
Apple Pie Bars	**158**
French Apple Cake	**160**
Sticky Toffee Pudding Cakes	**163**
Nutty Chocolate Fudge	**164**
Chocolate Pudding	**166**
Chocolate PB Nice Cream	**168**
Southern Peach Cobbler	**169**

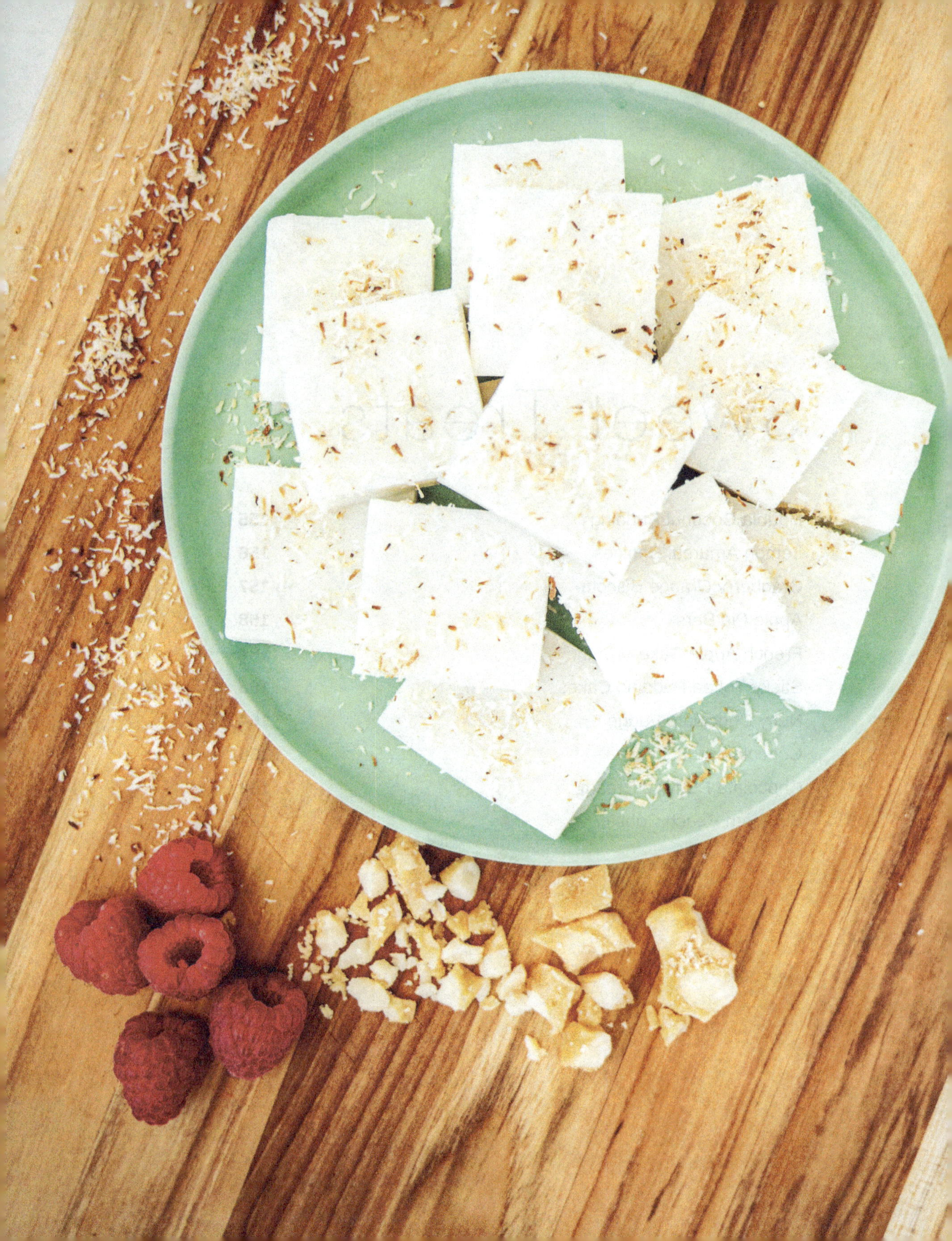

Haupia Coconut Pudding

A common dessert in Hawaii, Haupia is perfect for a warm summer night. It's a light and slightly sweet treat without too much sugar.

MAKES 14, 1 square per serving

1 can full fat coconut milk

1 cup unsweetened coconut milk from a carton

½ cup granulated white sugar

⅔ cup cornstarch or arrowroot starch

Pinch of salt

Topping Option

Toasted unsweetened coconut flakes

Spray an 8x8, 9x9, or 7x11 baking dish with cooking spray and set aside.

Add the canned coconut milk to a medium pot and bring to a simmer. Meanwhile in a mixing bowl, combine the unsweetened carton coconut milk, sugar, cornstarch, and salt and whisk together until cornstarch is dissolved.

Add the mixture to the pot with the hot coconut milk, whisking frequently as the mixture thickens. It will look like tapioca. Keep whisking until it is very thick and smooth.

Working carefully and quickly, pour into the baking dish and spread with a rubber spatula into an even layer.

Refrigerate for 2–3 hours, then cut into 12 squares. Top with toasted coconut.

COOKING TIP

Do not leave the mixture unattended during the cooking process. Make sure to whisk it frequently, especially after adding the mixture to the pot; this will help to remove the lumps and keep it from sticking to the pan.

Calories 66 | Carbs 12g | Fat 2g | Protein 0g | Fiber 0g | Sodium 6mg

Lemon Amaretti Cookies

This recipe has very minimal ingredients, but it does require a bit of technique. The base of these meringue-like cookies is aquafaba, the starchy liquid from a chickpea can. The aquafaba is whipped into peaks with cream of tartar, resulting in a simple replacement for a lot of egg whites.

MAKES 30-32, 1 cookie per serving

3 1/4 cups blanched almond flour

1 cup granulated white sugar

1/8 tsp salt

3/4 cup aquafaba (bean liquid) drained from canned chickpeas

1/4 tsp cream of tartar

1 tbsp lemon zest, optional

2 tsp lemon or almond extract

Lemon Glaze

1 cup powdered sugar

2 1/2 tbsp fresh lemon juice

Pinch of salt

Topping Option

Sliced almonds for the tops of the cookies before baking

Preheat oven to 325 degrees. Line a baking sheet with a silicone baking mat or parchment paper; set aside.

In a medium bowl, whisk together almond flour, sugar, and salt. Set aside.

In a large bowl, using a handheld mixer or stand mixer, whisk on high speed the aquafaba and cream of tartar until they hold peaks. Be patient as this will take about 8–10 minutes. Whisk in the lemon zest and lemon extract until just combined.

Gently fold in the almond flour mixture until well combined. Your dough should look like wet sand and almost dry.

Using a small tablespoon cookie scoop, portion cookie dough onto the baking sheet 1-inch apart. Clean off the outside of the scoop between cookies for a more uniform shape.

Bake for 25–30 minutes or until the bottom edges of the cookies are lightly golden. Remove from the oven and cool on the baking sheet before moving to a wire rack to cool completely.

Mix the glaze ingredients together in a bowl. It should be thick but able to drizzle. Drizzle the cooled cookies with the glaze and allow to set before serving.

COOKING TIP

If the cookies are sticking after baking, they may not have been baked enough to get golden on the bottom. To remove them without tearing the bottoms, allow cookies to cool on the baking sheet for 2 hours or overnight. Use a metal spatula to scrape them off easily.

Calories 74 | Carbs 10g | Fat 3g | Protein 2g | Fiber 2g | Sodium 20mg

Cranberry Orange Biscotti

I love biscotti around the holidays, but you don't have to wait until then to make these. These are a great addition to brunch or just to have as an after-dinner treat with something warm to drink. So much flavor is packed into these twice-baked cookies!

MAKES 16-20, 1 cookie per serving

- 1/3 cup unsweetened dairy-free or regular milk
- 1/2 cup neutral oil
- 1/2 cup granulated white sugar
- 1/4 cup powdered sugar
- Zest of one large orange
- 1 tsp vanilla extract
- 1 1/2 tsp baking powder
- 1/4 tsp sea salt
- 2 cups gluten-free or regular all-purpose flour
- 1/3 cup chopped low-sugar dried cranberries
- 1/4 cup sliced or slivered almonds
- 1/3 cup mini white or dark chocolate chips or a mix

Preheat the oven to 350 degrees and line a baking sheet with parchment or silicone baking mat.

In a large bowl, whisk together the milk, oil, sugars, zest, and vanilla. Add the baking powder and salt and stir again.

Add the flour and mix until half combined, then add the cranberries, almonds, and chocolate; and mix until well combined.

Transfer half of the dough to the counter and press together. Form into a 3x10-inch log shape. Transfer to the baking sheet. Repeat step with other half of dough.

Bake for 22 minutes. Remove from oven and allow to cool for 20 minutes on the baking sheet.

Transfer to a cutting board and using a serrated knife, cut 3/4-inches thick slices. Clean knife between slices as needed to keep chocolate from smearing. Arrange cookies on the baking sheet and bake again for 12 minutes. Allow to cool before serving.

Once cooled you can dip them in melted chocolate to decorate or just leave as is.

COOKING TIP

It is best to chop the dried cranberries into small pieces to help with cutting the cookie log without tearing the cookie. Also, this helps to reduce some of the chewiness from the cranberries baking for over 30 minutes.

Calories 189 | Carbs 20g | Fat 7g | Protein 2g | Fiber 2g | Sodium 50mg

Apple Pie Bars

This is an excellent alternative to getting that fall season pie fix. Use a tart green and a sweet red apple for a nice depth of flavor.

SERVES 12, about 3-inch square per serving

Filling

2 apples, peeled and sliced

1 tbsp maple syrup

2 tbsp brown or coconut sugar

2 tbsp lemon juice

2 tbsp all-purpose gluten-free or regular flour

1 tsp cinnamon

1/2 tbsp vanilla extract

Couple shakes of nutmeg

1/8 tsp ground cloves

1/8 tsp ground allspice

Crust

1 stick softened dairy-free or regular butter

1/3 cup brown or coconut sugar

1 cup all-purpose gluten-free or regular flour

1/4 cup old-fashioned oats

1/2 tsp cinnamon

Pinch of salt

Topping

1/3 cup brown or coconut sugar

1/2 cup dairy-free or regular butter, very soft or melted

1/2 cup old-fashioned oats

1/2 all-purpose gluten-free or regular flour

1/2 tsp cinnamon

2 tbsp chopped pecans or walnuts

Preheat the oven to 350 degrees and spray a 9x9 baking dish with cooking spray, then line with parchment paper.

In a medium mixing bowl, add all the filling ingredients and stir well to combine. Set aside.

To make the crust, add the butter and brown sugar to a large mixing bowl. Use a hand mixer to whip until fluffy. Add the flour, oats, cinnamon, and salt and mix again until the dough comes together in a crumbly but sticky dough. Press into the 9x9 baking dish and bake for 15 minutes. Allow bottom crust to cool for 20 minutes while you make the topping.

To make the topping, add all topping ingredients together in a bowl and mix together well.

Layer the apples with your hands on the bottom crust, then sprinkle with the topping. Gently press down with your hands. Bake for 45–50 minutes, rotating the baking dish halfway through.

Allow bars to cool completely in the refrigerator before removing from the pan or cutting. Cut into 12 bars and enjoy!

Calories 248 | Carbs 31g | Fat 13g | Protein 1g | Fiber 2g | Sodium 72mg

French Apple Cake (page 160)

French Apple Cake

I was introduced to this cake at a private cooking class. The host's mother-in-law sent me this hand-written recipe that I modified for a dessert class. It was love at first bite. One of my absolute favorite desserts, this one is a labor of love. Trust me when I say, it is so worth it.

SERVES 16, 1/4 of a cake per serving

Apples

12 cups peeled and sliced apples, 1/4-inch thick; approximately 9 - 10 medium apples, mix of red and green varieties

2 tbsp granulated white sugar

3 tsp rum or apple cider

1 tsp fresh lemon juice

Batter

3 eggs, room temperature

1 1/2 tsp vanilla extract

3/4 cup + 2 tbsp white sugar

1 1/2 tsp rum or apple cider

1 cup all-purpose regular flour

1 1/2 tsp baking powder

1/2 tsp salt

3/4 cup melted and cooled butter

1 tbsp granulated white sugar

Powdered sugar for dusting the finished cakes

Preheat the oven to 400 degrees and line two baking sheets with parchment paper.

Add the sliced apples, sugar, rum, and fresh lemon juice to a bowl and toss together. Let sit for 15 minutes.

Divide apples between the two baking sheets and spread out in a single layer. Bake for 20–30 minutes, gently tossing halfway through. Remove from oven and allow to cool for 20 minutes while preparing the batter. Reduce oven temperature to 375 degrees.

Line the bottom of four 4-inch springform mini pans with parchment and put it through the pan seam to keep the batter from coming out the bottom. Spray or butter the inside of each pan and coat with flour. Tap off excess flour.

To make the batter, add the eggs to a bowl and whisk well until foamy and pale, about 2 minutes. Add the vanilla, sugar, and rum and whisk again until smooth.

In another bowl, add the flour, baking powder, and salt and stir together. Add half the flour to the egg mixture and stir. Then add the butter and stir, finishing with the other half of the flour and stir together until just combined.

Instructions continued on next page...

Reserve 12 apple slices for the topping. Add the rest of the apples to the batter and fold in. Divide batter among the four mini pans and smooth out the top with an offset spatula or back of a spoon. Transfer to a baking sheet. Arrange three apple slices on the top of each cake and sprinkle the top with white sugar.

Bake for 50 minutes or until golden brown. If getting too dark on the top, cover with foil.

Remove from oven and gently use a paring knife to loosen around the edges of the cakes before they cool. Cool completely in the pans and then remove from pan. Dust the tops with powdered sugar and serve.

Sweet Treats

COOKING TIPS

These cakes can be made ahead and stored in the refrigerator for up to 5 days. Before serving, allow cakes to return to room temperature.

Don't be tempted to add more apple slices just because you already cut them. If you run low it is ok to use a little less, about 11 - 11 ½ cups. But adding more will weigh the cakes down and make them too wet in the middle.

Calories 229 | Carbs 34g | Fat 9g | Protein 3g | Fiber 3g | Sodium 228mg

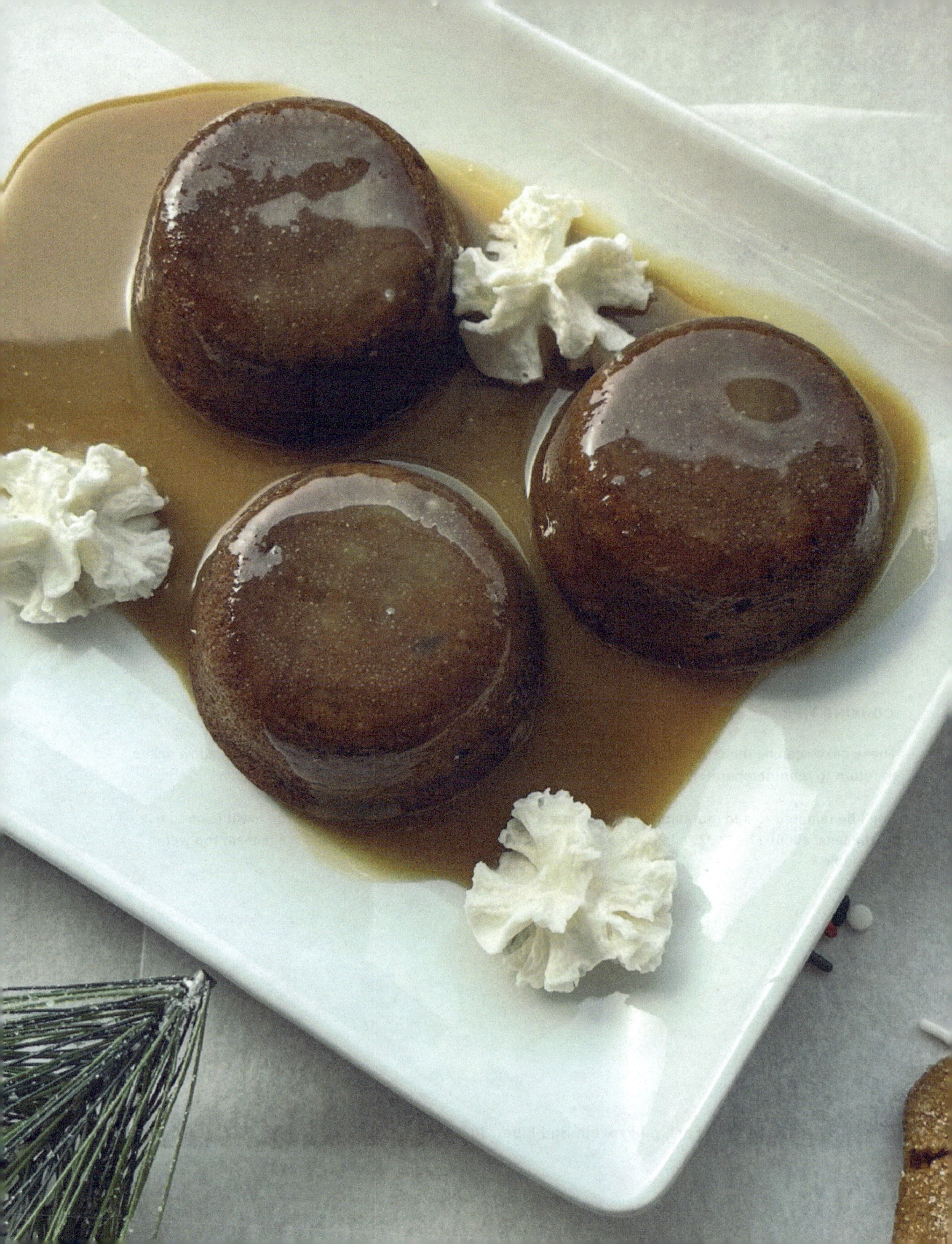

Sticky Toffee Pudding Cakes

Sticky Toffee Pudding is a traditional British dessert made around the holidays. What I love about these little cakes, is that they are made with natural sweeteners like dates, coconut sugar, and molasses. The toffee sauce, on the other hand, is the treat; use as much or as little as you like or omit if you need to.

SERVES 12, 1 cake per serving

Toffee Sauce

1/2 cup light brown sugar

1/2 cup dairy-free or regular heavy cream or full-fat canned coconut milk

1 tbsp dairy-free or regular butter

Pinch of salt

1/2 tbsp vanilla

Pudding

1 cup pitted Medjool dates, chopped

1 cup unsweetened milk or canned coconut milk

1/3 cup + 1 tbsp water

1 tsp baking soda

1/2 cup dairy-free or regular butter, room temperature

1/2 cup coconut sugar

1 tbsp molasses

1/2 tsp ground cinnamon

2 pinches ground nutmeg

1 1/4 cups all-purpose gluten-free or regular flour

For the toffee sauce, add the brown sugar, heavy cream, and butter of choice to a saucepan and simmer for 10 minutes, stirring often. Stir in the salt and vanilla extract and remove from heat. Transfer to a bowl or jar and let cool.

Preheat the oven to 375 degrees. For the pudding, add the dates, milk, and water to a saucepan and simmer for one minute on low heat. Remove from heat and add the baking soda. Mix together and let cool for 10 minutes.

In a mixing bowl, beat together the butter, sugar, and molasses. Slowly add the date mixture and mix well.

Add the cinnamon, nutmeg, and flour and fold in gently.

Transfer to 12 silicone muffin molds on a baking sheet or 12 greased muffin tin. Alternatively, you can also use six greased small ramekins.

Portion the pudding into the molds and bake for 20–22 minutes, until just cooked and a toothpick comes out clean.

Allow to cool slightly before handling. Transfer to a serving dish or individual plates and pour 1 - 2 tablespoons of the toffee sauce over the top of each pudding. Serve warm.

COOKING TIP

In the second step, it states to cook the dates in the liquid, then add the baking soda. The mixture should only be simmered for one minute before adding the teaspoon of baking soda. Any longer, and it will turn green and smell. The baking soda helps to break down the dates, but too much heat and moisture evaporation will create an unsightly mixture.

Calories 194 | Carbs 33g | Fat 7g | Protein 2g | Fiber 1g | Sodium 196mg

Nutty Chocolate Fudge

This Nutty Chocolate Fudge is a cross between fudge and a chocolate candy bar. Extra bonus, it's full of healthy nuts!

SERVES 24, 1 square per serving

3 cups semi-sweet chocolate chips

¼ cup coconut oil

⅓ cup peanut butter

1 tbsp maple syrup

24 pecan halves

Coarse salt for garnishing top

Grease a 7x11 or 8x8 baking dish, oil inside, and line with parchment. Set aside.

Add the chocolate chips, oil, peanut butter, and maple syrup to a medium saucepan or double boiler set to medium heat. Melt the ingredients and stir together until smooth.

Transfer to baking dish and top with pecan halves and coarse salt, if using. Refrigerate for 2 hours or overnight. Allow to sit on the counter for 10–20 minutes, then cut into squares.

Calories 189 | Carbs 19g | Fat 12g | Protein 1g | Fiber 3g | Sodium 60mg

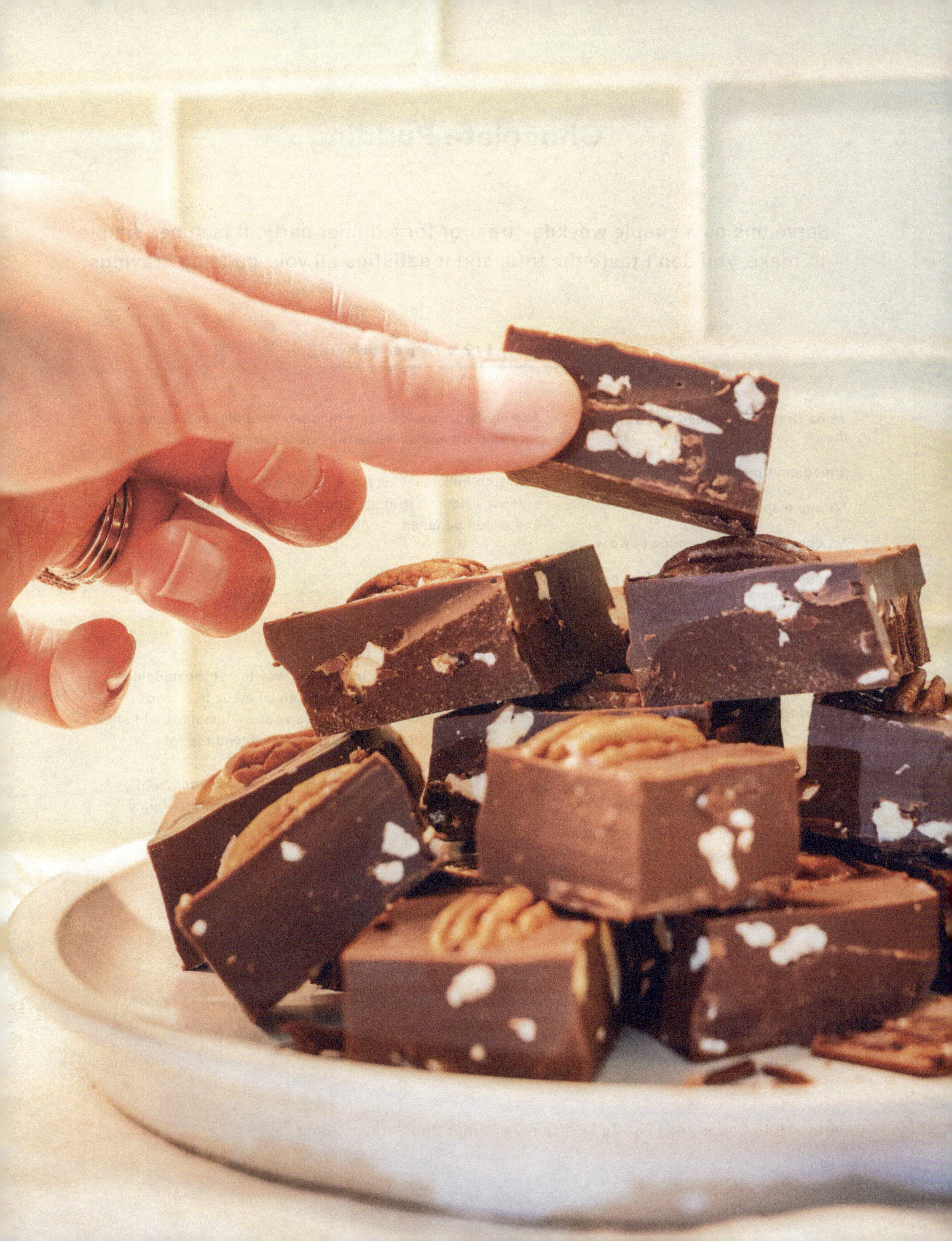

Chocolate Pudding

Serve this as a simple weekday treat or for a dinner party. It is super simple to make, you don't taste the tofu, and it satisfies all your pudding cravings.

SERVES 8, 1/2 cup per serving

16 oz firm tofu, drained and patted dry

1 medium ripe banana

1/2 cup maple syrup

2/3 cup unsweetened cocoa powder

1/2 cup unsweetened dairy-free or regular milk

1 tbsp vanilla extract

1/8 tsp salt

Toppings
Whipped cream of choice and sliced bananas

Add all the ingredients to a high-powered blender. Blend until very smooth and all white tofu pieces are gone.

Pour into individual serving cups or a bowl and refrigerate for at least 1 hour to firm up. Top each serving with whipped cream and sliced bananas.

COOKING TIPS

A high-powered blender is the best way to get the pudding smooth. If you don't have one, it can be made in a food processor. Just make sure to scrape down the sides and allow the machine to run long enough to fully blend the tofu.

You can also layer the pudding with sliced bananas, whipped cream of choice, and shaved chocolate on top for a fancy dessert!

Calories 154 | Carbs 24g | Fat 4g | Protein 7g | Fiber 3g | Sodium 93mg

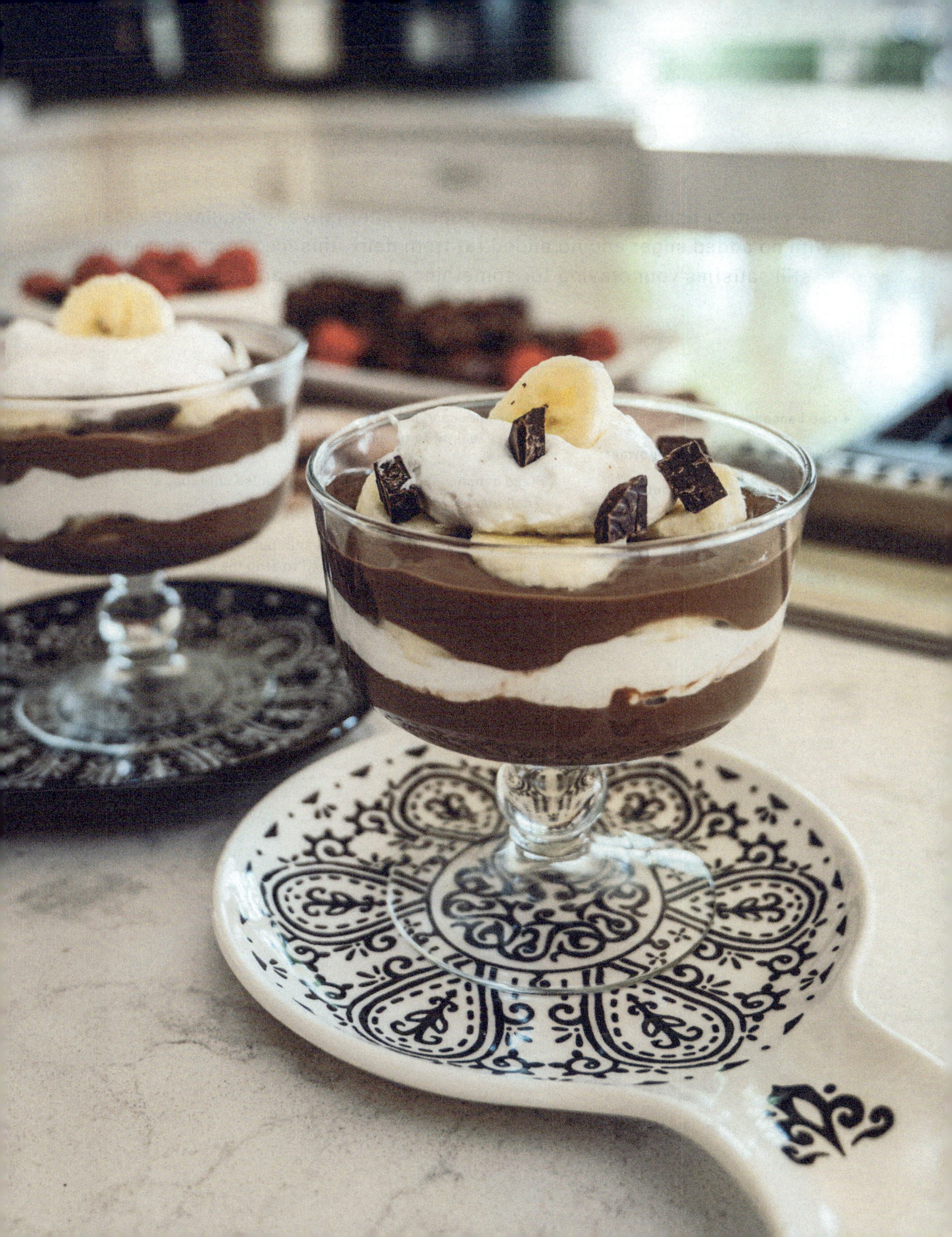

Chocolate PB Nice Cream

Nice cream or banana ice cream is a popular alternative to regular ice cream. With no added sugar and no added fat from dairy, this ice cream alternative still satisfies your craving for something cold and creamy on a hot day.

SERVES 4, 1/2 cup per serving

4 ripe bananas

2 tbsp unsweetened cocoa powder

1/4 cup powdered peanut butter

2 tbsp unsweetened dairy-free or regular milk

2 tbsp chopped peanuts

Remove peel and cut bananas into chunks. Place in freezer bag and freeze until firm, about 4–5 hours.

Place bananas in food processor and pulse until they are in small pieces.

Add cocoa powder, powdered peanut butter, and almond milk; blend until smooth. You may need to stop the processor to scrape down sides. Scoop into bowls, top with chopped peanuts, and serve.

Calories 159 | Carbs 21g | Fat 7g | Protein 4g | Fiber 3g | Sodium 76mg

Southern Peach Cobbler

This is a super simple cobbler recipe that's a reminder of what I grew up eating in the South. The biscuits are light and fluffy and melt right into the peaches with each bite.

SERVES 12, 3/4 cup per serving

Filling

Cooking spray

2 lbs frozen peaches defrosted or fresh peaches, peeled and sliced

1/4 cup maple syrup

1 tsp cinnamon

1 tbsp vanilla extract

1/2 tbsp cornstarch or arrowroot starch

Topping

1/2 cup brown sugar or coconut sugar

2/3 cup almond flour

1 cup all-purpose gluten-free or regular flour

2 tsp baking powder

1 tsp cinnamon

Couple pinches of salt

2 tbsp vanilla extract

1/2 cup coconut oil or dairy-free or regular butter, melted

1/2 cup unsweetened dairy-free or regular milk

2 tbsp brown sugar or coconut sugar for sprinkling on top

Preheat the oven to 400 degrees. Spray a 9x13 baking dish with cooking spray. Mix the filling ingredients together in a bowl. Pour filling into the baking dish and bake for 20 minutes.

For the topping, whisk together the sugar, flours, baking powder, cinnamon, and salt in a bowl. Add the vanilla, butter, and almond milk. Stir well to combine.

Dollop 12 small scoops of topping on the peaches, sprinkle the whole top with the 2 tablespoons of sugar, and bake for another 20–25 minutes. Let cool slightly before serving.

COOKING TIP

Placing the pan too close to the top of the oven for the second bake can darken the top of the cobbler too quickly. Bake on either the middle or bottom rack.

Calories 221 | Carbs 28g | Fat 10g | Protein 3g | Fiber 2g | Sodium 150mg

Acknowledgements

Chief Book Designer:
Alejandra Parra

Editors:
Chelsy Leslie, RDN, CD
Eva Lounsbury
Ineke Ojanen, RDN, CDCES
David Moon

Cover Designer:
Jordan Rowland

Foreword by:
Carol Taylor, MPH, RD, Certified Diabetes Care and Education Specialist, Health Coach

Photographers:
Caleb Rath, Photographer instagram.com/creeper.photos

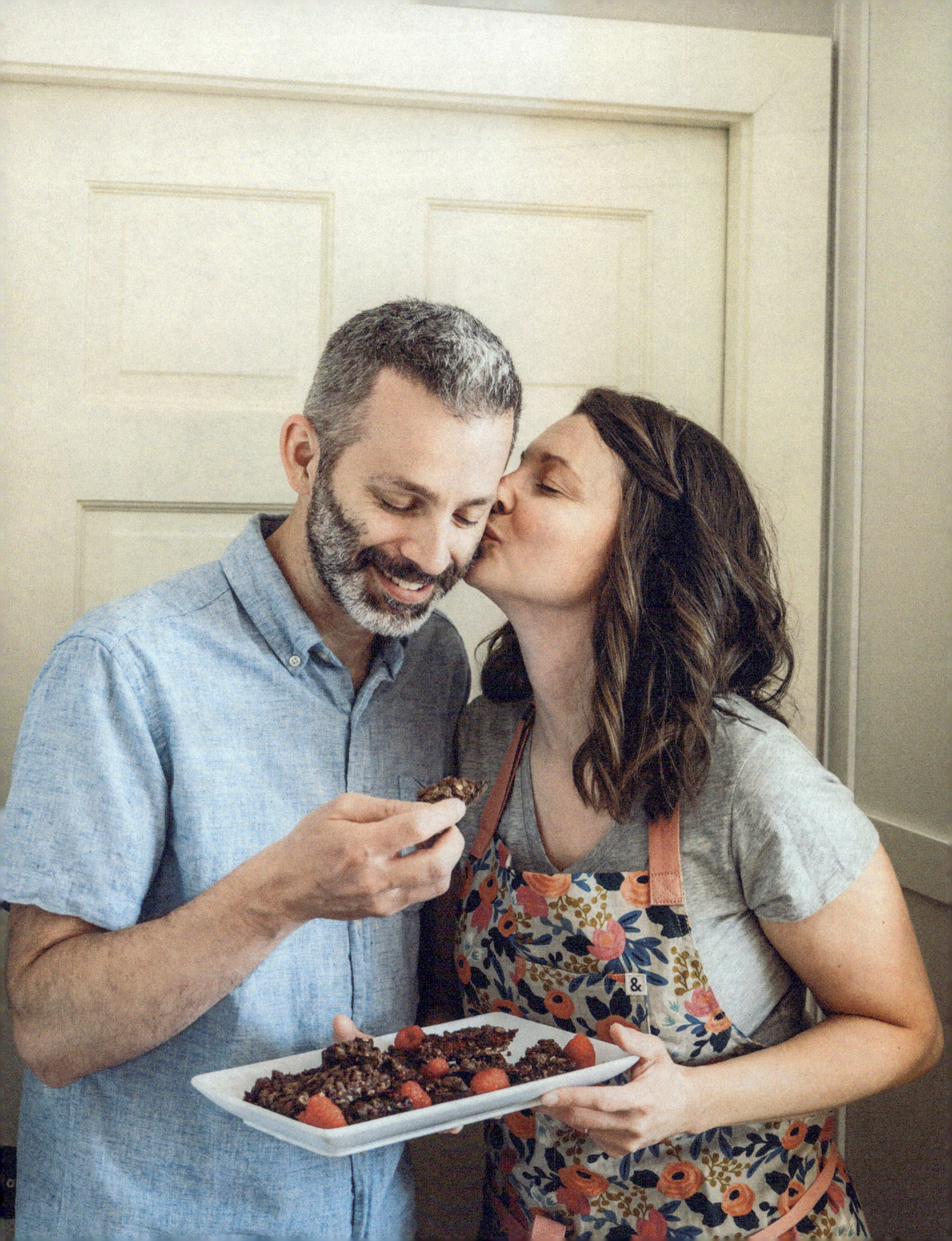

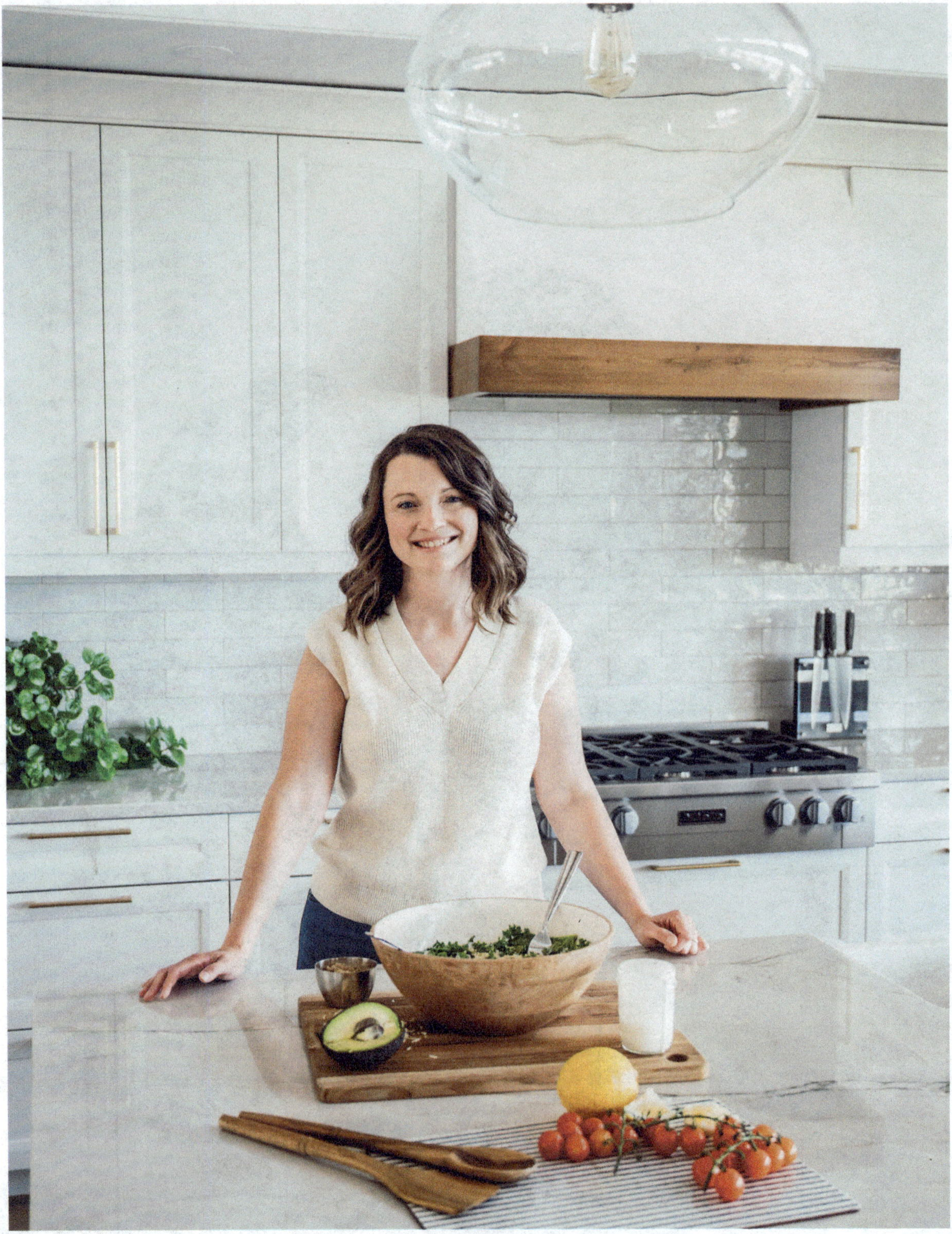

About the Author

**Elaina Moon, BS, ACE Certified Health Coach and Weight Management Specialist
Author, Owner Healthy Eats Nutrition Services and Cooking Classroom**

Elaina owns Healthy Eats Nutrition Services and Healthy Eats Classroom in Yakima, WA where she teaches cooking classes to the community and helps individuals implement healthy lifestyle changes. She is the Culinary Coordinator for Culinary Medicine Program with Central Washington University. Her first book, *Cooking Healthy,* inspired her to create this second book focused on family. She has a passion for creating delicious recipes and teaching her community how to eat healthier. Elaina loves to volunteer her time with local non-profit organizations when she is not spending time at her business or with her husband Dave, daughter Unique, and two rambunctious corgis Oliver and Hazel.

www.healthyeatsnutrition.com
Instagram: @healthy_eats_nutrition
Facebook: @healthyeatsnutrition